collector's guide to

Dolls
in
uniform

Joseph G. L. Bourgeois

COLLECTOR BOOKS
A Division of Schroeder Publishing Co., Inc.

The current values in this book should be used only as a guide. They are not intended to set prices, which vary from one section of the country to another. Auction prices as well as dealer prices vary greatly and are affected by condition as well as demand. Neither the Author nor the Publisher assumes responsibility for any losses that might be incurred as a result of consulting this guide.

SEARCHING FOR A PUBLISHER?

We are always looking for knowledgable people considered to be experts within their fields. If you feel that there is a real need for a book on your collectible subject and have a large comprehensive collection, contact Collector Books.

On the cover:

Top left; Item #7700. **G.I. Joe Action Marine.** White, brown molded hair, brown eyes. **$100.00 - 275.00 - 375.00. Nude: $50.00 - 75.00.** Top right; **W.A.V.E.** 15". Composition body. Articulated at hips and shoulders. Molded on W.A.V.E. hat. Tag: W.A.V.E. 1942. **$150.00 - 200.00 - 225.00. Nude: $150.00 - 200.00.**

Center: **John Wayne 7th Cavalry.** 17½". Plastic body. Vinyl head. Articulated. Blond molded hair. Painted blue eyes. Wearing the 7th Cavalry uniform. 1980. *(Courtesy of Arlene Vuono, The Doll Shop.)* **$25.00 - 75.00 - 135.00. Nude: $75.00 - 135.00.**

Bottom left; **G.I. Joe Race Car Driver uniform.** #5305. Uniform sold in plain plastic bags. Hasbro Ind. ca. 1968. **Uniform: $50.00 - 75.00 - 100.00.** Bottom center; **Barbie Police Officer.** 10688. 11½". Dressed in an authentic dark blue police officer's uniform. 1993. **$10.00 - 35.00 - 50.00.** Bottom right; **Sir Stuart the Silver Knight.** 11½". Plastic body. Black molded hair, moustache, goatee. Painted black eyes and silver molded on clothes. 1967. **$50.00 - 100.00 - 125.00.**

Book design by: Karen Long
Cover design by: Beth Summers

Printed by IMAGE GRAPHICS, INC., Paducah, Kentucky

≡ Acknowledgments ≡

I wrote this book because I thought it would be useful. I accept responsibility for any confusion, omissions, or errors. The best parts came from the sharing of information by many sensitive, unselfish, wonderful people. For those who have shared, encouraged, and have had an effect on this project I would like to acknowledge my gratitude, and extend a heartfelt thanks: Joseph John Bourgeois, Paul Stephen Bourgeois, Patricia R. Smith, Judith Radley, Roberta Schaffer, Harry G. Schreffler, Arlene Vuono.

CONTENTS

PRICING INFORMATION

Most dolls in this book have been given a value based on the following three categories:

CNP –   The doll is complete with its original outfit and accessories but no package.

MIP –   The doll is mint in its original package. The packaging may have some minor flaws.

PIP –   The pristine doll that has never been removed from its pristine packaging.

The suggested values will then read as follows: $25.00 – 50.00 – 65.00.

In certain cases such as in nude figures on those found in incomplete or played-with condition at yard sales, flea markets, and doll shows the suggested values will be given as a "range" of values. For example: $15.00 – 25.00.

Many factors determine value such as desirability, availability, condition, and completeness. Values may vary according to regions, seasons, etc. The values in this book should be used only as a guide. Neither the author nor the publisher assumes responsibility for any losses that might be incurred as a result of consulting this guide.

The *Dolls in Uniform* book begins at the time when G. I. Joe produced by the Hassenfeld Bros., Inc. first appeared and immediately captured the heart of the toy market. G. I. Joe's dominant position was challenged by many toy makers who produced 11½" articulated figures to compete in this volatile market. This book covers the major companies that produced dolls in uniform both before and during the G. I. Joe period. It was when these competing dolls in uniform appeared that they were quickly added to my collection. Older dolls in uniform observed at flea markets or at doll shows were noted and their characteristics were recorded.

It is easy enough to define the word uniform and use it as the chief criteria for inclusion in a book of this nature. But, there are many gray areas of uniforms. We certainly understand uniform when we see it on a nurse, policeman, or soldier. But, defining uniform when we see it on a space alien becomes more difficult. So, the author has decided it is better to err in the inclusion of the uniformed doll than to err in the exclusion of the uniformed doll. It should be noted that while many toys have authentically styled uniforms such as the "Mechanical Soldier" (which is illustrated below), they are not the focus of this book. One-of-a-kind dolls have also been excluded even though the uniform may be very authentic.

6", **U. S. Army Sergent**, mechanical metal man. Chein Co. 1940's.

$150.00 - 200.00.

ALEXANDER DOLL COMPANY
#317, **Wendy**, Girl Scout. 8".
Vinyl body. Articulated at hips,
shoulders, and neck. Rooted
brown hair. Blue sleep eyes.
Mark: Alexander Doll Co. 1991.

$35.00 – 50.00.

A. C. GILBERT COMPANY
#16130, **Moon McDare, Action Spaceman.** 12". Plas-
tic body. Vinyl head. Articulated at hips, shoulders, and
neck. Brown molded hair. Painted brown eyes. Mark on
head: G. Mark on back: 2. Mark inside left arm near
armpit: 118K. Mark inside right arm near armpit: 78K.
Dressed in a blue space-type jumpsuit with tag: McDare
/ A.C. Gilbert Co. / Japan 1966.

$25.00 – 75.00 – 100.00.

=== DOLLS NOT PICTURED ===

ALEXANDER DOLL COMPANY
W. A. A. C. 14". Composition body. Articulated at hips, shoulders, neck. Glued on
mohair wig. Brown sleep eyes. Mark on head: Mme. Alexander. Mark on tag: W. A. A. C.
/ Madame Alexander / New York / All rights reserved. 1942.

$50.00 – 200.00 – 250.00.

W. A. V. E. 14". Composition body. Articulated at hips, shoulders, neck. Glued on wig.
Blue sleep eyes. Mark on head: Mme. Alexander. Mark on tag: W. A. V. E. / Madame
Alexander / New York / All rights reserved. 1942.

$50.00 – 200.00 – 250.00.

W. A. A. F. 14". Composition body. Articulated at hips, shoulders, neck. Glued on wig.
Sleep eyes. Mark on head: Mme. Alexander. Mark on tag: W. A. A. F. / Madame
Alexander / New York / All rights reserved. 1942.

$50.00 – 200.00 – 250.00.

Mary Martin sailor suit. 14". Hard plastic body. Articulated at hips, shoulders, neck. Glued
on wig. Sleep eyes. Mark on tag on clothes: Mary Martin / Madame Alexander. 1949.

$100.00 – 300.00 – 500.00.

ALEXANDER DOLL COMPANY
Wendy. 8". Majorette. #314,
Alexander Doll Co. 1991 (Courtesy of
Arlene Vuono. The Doll Shop).

$35.00 – 50.00.

=== DOLLS NOT PICTURED ===

AMERICAN CHARACTER DOLL COMPANY

Hostess American Airlines. 12". Adult female plastic body. Articulated at hips, shoulders, and neck. Rooted blonde hair. Painted right-looking blue eyes. High heel feet. Marks: none. 1970's.

$10.00 – 25.00 – 50.00.

ARRANBEE DOLL COMPANY

Female Army Soldier. 16". Stuffed cloth body with attached composition head, arms, and legs. Blonde molded hair. Painted blue eyes. Olive drab uniform with Lincoln head brass buttons. Marks: none. 1930's. *(Courtesy Patricia R. Smith, Modern Dollector's Dolls #4, pg 35.)*

$65.00 – 100.00.

AVERILL MANUFACTURING COMPANY – GEORGENE DIV.

Brownie. 13". Cloth stuffed body. Blonde mohair hair. Painted features with right-looking blue eyes. Authentically styled Brownie uniform of the period. 1949. *(Courtesy of Roberta Schaffer, Girl Scout Museum, Taunton, MA.)*

$50.00 – 75.00.

BEEHLER ARTS LTD.

Lucy (Virga) Brownie. 8". Hard plastic body. Vinyl head. Articulated at hips, shoulders, and neck. Brown glued on wig over molded hair. Feet have molded on T-strap shoes. Deep indentation under lower lip. Mark on head: Virga. 1959.

$25.00 – 50.00.

Lucy (Virga) Girl Scout. 8". Hard plastic body. Vinyl head. Description same as Lucy (Virga) Brownie except for blonde glued on wig. (Note: Socks and shoes fit on easily over the molded T-strap shoes.) 1960.

$25.00 – 50.00.

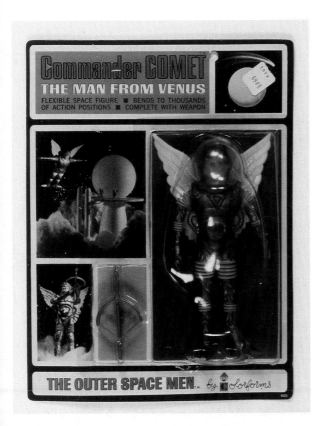

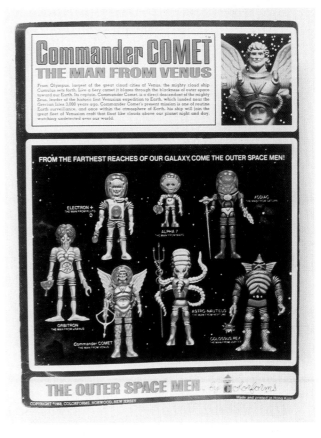

COLORFORMS   *The Outer Space Men*

Commander Comet (Venus). 6". Molded on space uniform. Soft plastic body with limbs concealing a wire which permits easy flexing and posing at the accordion joints of the figure. White wings. (Only Commander Comet has wings.) 1968.

$100.00 – 200.00 – 250.00.

COLORFORMS   *The Outer Space Men*

Commander Comet (Venus). Package back.

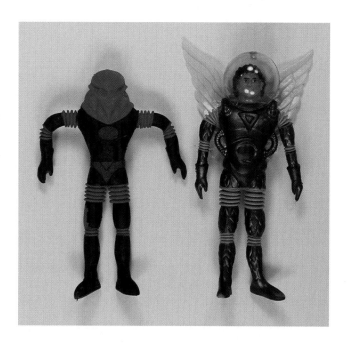

COLORFORMS   *The Outer Space Men*

Alpha 7 (Mars). 6" Molded on space uniform. Soft plastic body with limbs concealing a wire which permits easy flexing and posing at the accordion joints of the figure. 1968.

$80.00 – 200.00 – 250.00.

Astro Nautilus (Neptune). 6". Description same as Alpha 7.

$120.00 – 200.00 – 250.00.

Colossus Rex (Jupiter). 6". Description same as Alpha 7.

$90.00 – 200.00 – 250.00.

Electron + (Pluto). 6". Description same as Alpha 7.

$90.00 – 200.00 – 250.00.

Orbitron (Uranus). 6". Description same as Alpha 7.

$90.00 – 200.00 – 250.00.

COLORFORMS   *The Outer Space Men*

Zodiac (Saturn). 6". Molded on space uniform. Soft plastic body with limbs concealing a wire which permits easy flexing and posing at the accordion joints of the figure. 1968.

$80.00 – 200.00 – 250.00.

COSMOPOLITAN DOLL & TOY COMPANY

#331 Ginger Girl Scout. 8" Ginger in Girl Scout uniform #331. Hard plastic body. Vinyl head. Articulated at hips, shoulders, and neck. Blonde glued on wig. Blue sleep eyes with plastic eyelashes. Mark on head: Ginger. 1956. (Note: Plastic head has no mark, 1955. Vinyl head is marked Ginger, from 1956 on.)

$25.00 –50.00.

#332 Ginger Brownie. 8". Ginger in Brownie uniform #332. Description same as Ginger Girl Scout. 1955, 1956.

$25.00 –50.00.

#335 Ginger Nurse. 8". Ginger in white nurse's uniform #335. Description same as Ginger Girl Scout. 1955, 1956.

$25.00 –50.00.

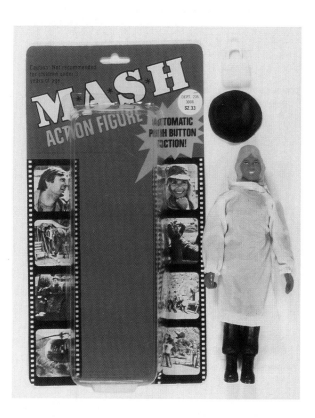

DURHAM INDUSTRIES, INC.

Major Houlihan (Hot Lips). 9". Nurse in "M. A. S. H." TV series. Plastic body. Molded blonde hair. Painted blue eyes. Molded on fatigue uniform. Mark on back: Durham Industries Inc./ N.Y., NY 10010. / Made in Hong Kong No. 3008 / © Durham Industries Inc. / 1975 all rights reserved.

$10.00 – 35.00 – 45.00.

Durham Industries, Inc.
Captain Pierce (Hawkeye). 9". Doctor in "M .A. S. H." TV series. Plastic body. Molded black hair. Painted blue eyes. Molded on fatigue uniform. Mark on back: Durham Industries Inc./ N.Y., NY 10010. / Made in Hong Kong No. 3008 / © Durham Industries Inc. / 1975 all rights reserved.
$10.00 ~ 35.00 ~ 45.00.

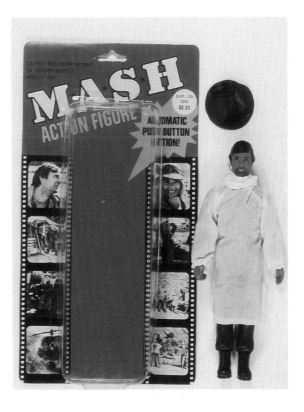

====== Dolls Not Pictured ======

Durham Industries, Inc.
B. J. Hunnicut. 9". Doctor in "M. A. S. H." TV series. Characteristics same as Captain Pierce except: face and blond molded hair. 1975.
$10.00 ~ 35.00 ~ 45.00.

#3062 Safari Hunter. 5¾". Plastic body. Vinyl head. Characteristics same as Safari Hunter Policeman. 1975.
$10.00 ~ 15.00 ~ 20.00.

Durham Industries, Inc.
#3003 Cycle Cop. 5¾". All plastic body. Vinyl head with molded on white helmet. Molded on blue motorcycle policeman uniform. Molded on black boots. Spring loaded right arm that raises by push button. Mark on shoulders: Durham Ind. Inc. / New York, N. Y. 10010. Mark on mid-back: Made in Hong Kong No. 3003 / Design reg. No. 965717. 1975.
$10.00 ~ 15.00 ~ 20.00.

Durham Industries, Inc.
#3004 **Ranger Army.** 5¾". Characteristics same as Cycle Cop
except: molded on green helmet, green army combat uniform, and black boots. 1975.

$10.00 – 15.00 – 20.00.

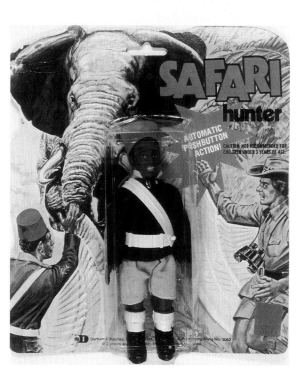

Durham Industries, Inc.
#3062 Safari Hunter Policeman.
5¾". Brown plastic body. Brown vinyl
head. Articulated at hips, shoulders,
and neck. Black molded hair. Painted
black eyes. Spring loaded right arm
which raises by push button. Mark on
lower back: Durham Ind. / New York.
N.Y. 10010 / Made in Hong Kong /
Item No. 3005. 1975.

$10.00 – 15.00 – 20.00.

========= DOLLS NOT PICTURED =========

EDICO
Adventurer. 11½". Plastic body. Molded brown hair. Painted blue eyes. Original outfit: floral swim trunks. Figure designed to use G.I. Joe and other action figure accessories. Mark on back: Made in / Hong Kong. 1974.
$10.00 – 25.00 – 30.00.

EEGEE
Andy Airline Pilot. 12". Plastic body. Vinyl head and arms. Articulated at hips, shoulders, and neck. Blond molded hair. Painted right-looking blue eyes. Mark on head: EG – 1961. Mark on lower back: EG – 1961. Original outfit: airline pilot uniform.
$10.00 – 25.00 – 50.00.

©EFFANBEE DOLL COMPANY
Fluffy Official Brownie. 8". Fluffy in an official Brownie Girl Scout Uniform of the period. Soft vinyl body. Articulated at hips, shoulders, and neck. Brown rooted hair. Blue sleep eyes. Mark on head: Effanbee / 19©65 or Fluffy. Missing hat and orange tie. 1965.
$25.00 –50.00 – 75.00.

©EFFANBEE DOLL COMPANY
General Eisenhower U. S. Army Officer. 16". Plastic body. Vinyl head. Articulated. Light brown molded hair. Painted blue eyes. U.S. Army officer's uniform. 1987. *(Courtesy of Arlene Vuono, The Doll Shop.)*
$25.00 – 75.00 – 135.00.

©EFFANBEE DOLL COMPANY
John Wayne 7th Cavalry. 17½". Plastic body. Vinyl head. Articulated. Blond molded hair. Painted blue eyes. Wearing the 7th Cavalry uniform. 1980. *(Courtesy of Arlene Vuono, The Doll Shop.)*
$25.00 – 75.00 – 135.00.

======= DOLLS NOT PICTURED =======

©EFFANBEE DOLL COMPANY

Skippy™ Soldier. 14". Skippy in WWII soldier uniform. Composition head with brown molded hair, arms, and legs with molded on shoes. Stuffed cloth body. Mark: Effanbee / Skippy / © / P. L. Crosby. 1942.
$25.00 ~ 100.00 ~ 150.00.

Skippy™ Sailor. 14". Skippy in WWII navy uniform. Description same as Skippy Soldier. 1942.
$25.00 ~ 100.00 ~ 150.00.

Skippy™ Air Force Pilot. 14". Skippy in WWII aviator uniform. Description same as Skippy Soldier. 1942.
$25.00 ~ 100.00 ~ 150.00.

Mickey Sailor. 11". All-American boy in sailor uniform. All plastic body. Articulated at hips, shoulders, and neck. Molded on navy hat. Painted molded hair. Painted blue eyes. Mark on head: Mickey / Effanbee, or just Effanbee. 1956.
$25.00 ~ 100.00 ~ 150.00.

Mickey Air Cadet. 11". Mickey in aviator uniform. Description same as Mickey Sailor except molded on aviator cap. 1957.
$25.00 ~ 100.00 ~ 150.00.

Mickey Johnny Reb. 11". Mickey in Confederate army uniform. Description same as Mickey Sailor except molded on Confederate army cap. 1957.
$25.00 ~ 100.00 ~ 150.00.

Mickey Yankee Boy. 11". Mickey in Union army uniform. Description same as Mickey Sailor except molded on Union army cap. 1957.
$25.00 ~ 100.00 ~ 150.00.

Mickey Soldier. 11". Mickey in WWII army uniform. Description same as Mickey Sailor except molded on army cap. 1957.
$25.00 ~ 100.00 ~ 150.00.

Mickey Marine. 11" Mickey in WWII marine uniform. Description same as Mickey Sailor except molded on marine cap. 1957.
$25.00 ~ 100.00 ~ 150.00.

Mickey Fireman. 11". Mickey in fireman uniform. Description same as Mickey Sailor except molded on fireman hat. 1957.
$25.00 ~ 50.00 ~ 150.00.

Mickey Policeman. 11". Mickey in policeman uniform. Description same as Mickey Sailor except for molded on policeman hat. 1957.
$25.00 ~ 50.00 ~ 150.00.

Mickey Boy Scout. 11". Mickey in American Boy Scout uniform. Description same as Mickey Sailor except for molded on Boy Scout hat. 1957. **$25.00 ~ 100.00 ~ 150.00.**

Mickey Cub Scout. 11". Mickey in Cub Scout uniform of the period. Description same as Mickey Sailor except for molded on Cub Scout cap. 1957.
$25.00 ~ 100.00 ~ 150.00.

Patsy Ann™ Girl Scout. 15". Patsy Ann in official Girl Scout uniform. Plastic body. Articulated at hips (some at the waist), shoulders, and neck. Blonde rooted hair. Blue sleep eyes. Mark on head: Effanbee / Patsy Ann / © 1959.
$50.00 ~ 100.00 ~ 125.00.

Alyssa Girl Scout. 15". Alyssa in a Girl Scout uniform. Plastic body. Articulated at hips, shoulders, and neck. Blonde rooted hair. Blue sleep eyes. 1962.
$50.00 ~ 100.00 ~ 125.00.

Alyssa Brownie. 15". Alyssa in a Brownie uniform. Description same as Alyssa Girl Scout except brown rooted hair. 1962.
$50.00 ~ 100.00 ~ 125.00.

Alyssa Camp Fire Girl. 15". Alyssa in a Camp Fire Girl uniform. Description same as Alyssa Girl Scout. 1962.
$50.00 ~ 100.00 ~ 125.00.

Alyssa Blue Bird. 15". Alyssa in a Blue Bird uniform. Description same as Alyssa Girl Scout 1962.
$50.00 ~ 100.00 ~ 125.00.

Suzette™ Girl Scout. 15". Suzette in a Girl Scout uniform. Plastic teen style body. Articulated at hips, shoulders, and neck. Blonde rooted hair with full bangs. Blue sleep eyes. 1965.
$50.00 ~ 100.00 ~ 125.00.

Suzette™ Brownie. 15". Suzette in a Brownie uniform. Description same as Suzette Girl Scout except brown rooted hair. 1965.
$50.00 ~ 100.00 ~ 125.00.

Suzette™ Camp Fire Girl. 15". Suzette in Camp Fire Girl uniform. Description same as Suzette Girl Scout. 1965.
$50.00 ~ 100.00 ~ 125.00.

Suzette™ Blue Bird. 15". Suzette in a Blue Bird uniform. Description same as Suzette Girl Scout. 1965.
$50.00 ~ 100.00 ~ 125.00.

Fluffy Official Cadette Girl Scout. 11". Fluffy in the official Cadette Girl Scout uniform. Soft vinyl body. Articulated at hips, shoulders, and neck. Blonde rooted hair. Blue sleep eyes. Mark on head: Effanbee / 1963.
$25.00 ~ 50.00 ~ 75.00.

Fluffy Blue Bird. 10". Fluffy in Blue Bird uniform. Soft vinyl body. Articulated at hips, shoulders, and neck. Brown rooted hair.

Blue sleep eyes. Mark on head: F & B / 1964 in a circle. 1964.

$25.00 – 50.00 – 75.00.

Fluffy Official Girl Scout. 8". Fluffy in an official Girl Scout uniform of the period. Soft vinyl body. Articulated at hips, shoulders, and neck. Blonde rooted hair. Blue sleep eyes. Mark on head: Effanbee / 19©65 or Fluffy.

$25.00 – 50.00 – 75.00.

Fluffy Blue Bird. 8". Fluffy in a Blue Bird uniform. Description sam as 8" Fluffy Official Brownie. 1965.

$25.00 – 50.00 – 75.00.

Fluffy Camp Fire Girl. 8". Fluffy in a Campfire Girl uniform. Description same as 8" Fluffy Official Brownie. 1965.

$25.00 – 50.00 – 75.00.

Fluffy Official Girl Scout. 11½". Fluffy in an Official Girl Scout uniform consisting of a green jumper with a green trefoil patterned striped white blouse. Green socks. Brown shoes. Green beany style hat with the Girl Scout logo. Vinyl body. Articulated at hips, shoulders, and neck. Brown rooted hair. Blue sleep eyes. Mark on head: Effanbee / 1974.

$50.00 – 100.00 – 125.00.

Fluffy Official Brownie. 11½". Fluffy in an official Brownie uniform consisting of a brown jumper with a brown patterned striped white blouse. Brown socks. Brown shoes. Brown beany style hat with the Brownie logo. Description same as 11½" Fluffy Official Girl Scout except for blonde rooted hair. 1974.

$50.00 – 100.00 – 125.00.

ELITE CREATIONS

Fighting Ace. 12" Plastic body. Articulated at hips, shoulders, and neck. Black molded hair. Painted blue eyes. Mark on back: Made in / Hong Kong / 2012. ca. 1970.

$10.00 – 25.00 – 30.00.

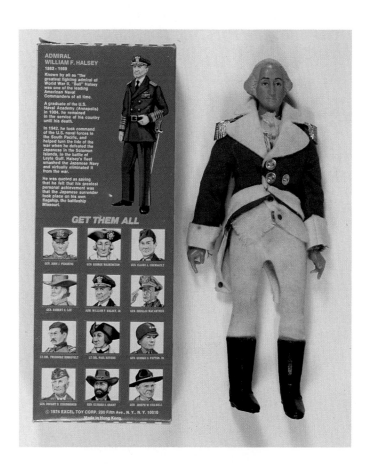

EXCEL TOY CORP.

#501. General George Washington. 9½". Plastic body. Articulated at ankles, knees, hips, waist, shoulders, elbows, wrist, and neck. Gray molded hair. Brown painted eyes. Mark on back: © Excel Toy Corp / Made in Hong Kong. 1974.

$20.00 – 75.00 – 100.00.

EXCEL TOY CORP.

#502. Lt. Col. Paul Revere. 9½". Plastic body. Description same as Washington except face and light brown molded hair. Painted brown eyes. 1974.

$20.00 – 75.00 – 100.00.

EXCEL TOY CORP.
#503. Gen. Ulysses S. Grant. 9½". Plastic body. Description same as Washington except face and black molded hair and beard. 1974.
$20.00 ~ 75.00 ~ 100.00.

EXCEL TOY CORP.
#504. Gen. Robert E. Lee. 9½". Plastic body. Description same as Washington except face and gray molded hair and beard. 1974.
$20.00 ~ 75.00 ~ 100.00.

EXCEL TOY CORP.
#505. Lt. Col. Theodore Roosevelt. 9½". Plastic body. Description same as Washington except face and dark brown hair and moustashe. 1974.
$20.00 ~ 75.00 ~ 100.00.

EXCEL TOY CORP.
#507. Gen. Claire L. Chennault. 9½". Plastic body. Description same as Washington except face and brown molded hair. 1974.

$20.00 – 75.00 – 100.00.

EXCEL TOY CORP.
#506. Gen. John J. Pershing. 9½". Plastic body. Description same as Washington except face and light brown molded hair and moustache. 1974.

$20.00 – 75.00 – 100.00.

EXCEL TOY CORP.
#508. Gen. Douglas MacArthur. 9½". Plastic body. Description same as Washington except face and light brown molded hair. 1974.

$20.00 – 75.00 – 100.00.

EXCEL TOY CORP.
#509. Gen. Joseph W. Stilwell. 9½". Plastic body. Description same as Washington except face and blond molded hair. 1974.

$20.00 – 75.00 – 100.00.

EXCEL TOY CORP.
#510. Adm. William F. Halsey. 9½". Plastic body. Description same as Washington except face, black molded hair, and painted blue eyes. 1974.

$20.00 – 75.00 – 100.00.

EXCEL TOY CORP.
#511. Gen. Dwight D. Eisenhower. 9½". Plastic body. Description same as Washington except face, blond molded hair, and painted blue eyes. 1974.

$20.00 – 75.00 – 100.00.

Excel Toy Corp.
#512. Gen. George S. Patton. 9½". Plastic body. Description same as Washington except face and brown molded hair. 1974.
$20.00 – 75.00 – 100.00.

Freundlich Novelty Company
W. A. V. E. 15". Composition body. Articulated at hips and shoulders. Molded on W. A. V. E. hat. Tag: W. A. V. E. 1942.
$150.00 – 200.00 – 225.00.

══════ Dolls Not Pictured ══════

Freundlich Novelty Company
General Douglas MacArthur. 16". Composition body. Articulated at hips, shoulders. Molded on officer's hat. Dressed in army officer's uniform. Tag: General MacArthur — Man of the hour. Freundlich Novelty Company. 1942.
$150.00 – 200.00 – 215.00.

Sailor. 15". Composition body. Articulated at hips and shoulders. Molded on sailor hat. Painted features. 1942.
$150.00 – 200.00 – 225.00.

Soldier. 15". Composition body. Articulated at hips and shoulders. Molded on army hat. Painted features. Tag: Praise the Lord and pass the ammunition. 1942.
$150.00 – 200.00 – 225.00.

W. A. A. C. 15". Composition body. Articulated at hips and shoulders. Painted features. Tag: W. A. A. C. Molded on W. A. A. C. hat. 1942.
$150.00 – 200.00 – 225.00.

FUN-WORLD INC.   *The Collectors Series of Great Americans*
George Washington. 8". Plastic body. Fully articulated.
Gray molded hair. Painted brown eyes. Mark on back:
Made in / Hong Kong. 1976.

$10.00 ~ 35.00 ~ 50.00.

FUN-WORLD INC.   *The Collectors Series of Great Americans*
Abraham Lincoln. 8". Plastic body. Fully articulated. Black molded
hair and beard. Mark on back: Made in / Hong Kong. 1976.

$10.00 ~ 35.00 ~ 50.00.

FUN-WORLD INC.   *The Collectors Series of Great Americans*
Uncle Sam. 8". Plastic body. Fully articulated. Gray molded hair
and goatee. Painted brown eyes. Mark on back: Made in / Hong
Kong. 1976.

$10.00 ~ 35.00 ~ 50.00.

GABRIEL INDUSTRIES INC.— HUBLEY DIVISION   *The Lone Ranger Rides Again Series*

7th Cavalry Officer's Uniform. The cellophane window package titled "The Lost Cavalry Patrol" includes: dark blue officer's campaign hat, dark blue officer's dress jacket, light blue cavalry pants with yellow stripe, black cavalry boots with spurs, pistol and belted pistol holster, cavalry carbine, binocular with case, saber with scabbard, ammo pouch, bugle, 7th cavalry red and white flag, and small *Lone Ranger* comic book. 1978.

$10.00 – 45.00 – 55.00.

GIRL SCOUT DOLLS

Girl Scout dolls may be divided into five general categories.

1) The Girl Scout dolls that are called the "Official Girl Scout Doll" of a particular period and sold through the Girl Scout equipment catalog. These dolls reflect an authentic uniform of the period. These dolls are manufactured by companies licensed by the Girl Scout organization.

2) Girl Scout dolls which are look-alikes of the official doll, but with small differences in their uniforms of the period. They are manufactured by companies that are either sanctioned or unknown by the Girl Scout organization.

3) Dolls that are dressed in "Official Girl Scout uniforms or Brownie uniforms" which are sold in accessory packages manufactured by companies licensed by the Girl Scout organization.

4) Dolls that are dressed in very accurate and authentic Girl Scout uniforms made of the same uniform fabrics as the official uniforms. The uniforms are homemade with excellent skill on the part of the maker. These dolls may be one of a kind.

5) Very large dolls such as the 40" tall dolls that are dressed in official size 5 Girl Scout or Brownie uniforms. These small official uniforms may have been tailored to fit the large doll.

The following listed companies made dolls dressed in Girl Scout and Brownie uniforms. Several of them also made separate accessory packages containing Girl Scout, Brownie, as well as Blue Bird, and Camp Fire Girl uniforms. (Look in the sections with the company name in this book.)

Alexander Doll Company	Averill Manufacturing Co.
Beehler Arts Ltd.	Cosmopolitan Doll & Toy Co.
Effanbee Doll Company	Norma Originals Inc.
Terri Lee Doll Company	Vogue Doll Inc.

GIRL SCOUT DOLLS
1912 (replica) Girl Scout uniform, cloth doll. 12". 1986 Burry Cookie Premium. *(Courtesy of Roberta Schaffer, Girl Scout Museum, Taunton, MA.)*

$25.00 – 50.00.

GIRL SCOUT DOLLS
1919 Adult uniform for Girl Scout leader. 6½". Cloth doll. Hallmark Co. 1979. *(Courtesy of Roberta Schaffer, Girl Scout Museum, Taunton, MA.)*

$25.00 – 50.00.

GIRL SCOUT DOLLS
Sylvia 1940 Intermediate Girl Scout uniform. 14". Cloth doll. Mfg. Unk. *(Courtesy of Roberta Schaffer, Girl Scout Museum, Taunton, MA.)*
$50.00 – 75.00.

GIRL SCOUT DOLLS
1949 Brownie uniform. 13". Cloth doll. Georgene Novelties, Inc. — Division of Averill Dolls. ca. 1949. *(Courtesy of Roberta Schaffer, Girl Scout Museum, Taunton, MA.)*
$50.00 – 75.00.

GIRL SCOUT DOLLS
Fluffy 1968 Girl Scout uniform. 8".
©Effanbee Doll Co. 1968. *(Courtesy of Roberta Schaffer, Girl Scout Museum, Taunton, MA.)*

$50.00 – 65.00.

GIRL SCOUT DOLLS
1940 Intermediate Girl Scout uniform. 7½". Plastic doll. (1950)
Norma Originals Inc. *(Courtesy of Roberta Schaffer, Girl Scout Museum, Taunton, MA.)*

$50.00 – 65.00.

GIRL SCOUT DOLLS
Fluffy. 8". **1965 Girl Scout uniform**. ©Effanbee Doll Co. 1965. *(Courtesy of Roberta Schaffer, Girl Scout Museum, Taunton, MA.)*

$50.00 – 65.00.

1975 Girl Scout uniform for 13" cloth doll. Mfg. Unk. *(Courtesy of Roberta Schaffer, Girl Scout Museum, Taunton, MA).*
$25.00 – 30.00.

Fluffy. 8". 1960 Brownie uniform. ©Effanbee Doll Co. ca. 1960. *(Courtesy of Roberta Schaffer, Girl Scout Museum, Taunton, MA.)*
$35.00 – 40.00.

Ginger. 7½". 1956 Brownie uniform. Cosmopolitan Doll Co. ca 1956. *(Courtesy of Roberta Schaffer, Girl Scout Museum, Taunton, MA.)*
$35.00 – 45.00.

Fluffy. 8". 1965 Brownie uniform. ©Effanbee Doll Co. 1965. Note: Difference from 1960 Fluffy. *(Courtesy of Roberta Schaffer, Girl Scout Museum, Taunton, MA.)*
$35.00 – 45.00.

Brownie. 13". 1975 Brownie uniform. Cloth Doll. Mfg. Unk. ca. 1986. *(Courtesy of Roberta Schaffer, Girl Scout Museum, Taunton, MA.)*
$35.00 – 45.00.

GIRL SCOUT DOLLS
1994 Brownie uniform for 13" cloth doll. No hat included. Dolls Delights Inc. 1994. *(Courtesy of Roberta Schaffer, Girl
Scout Museum, Taunton, MA.)*

$25.00 – 35.00.

GIRL SCOUT DOLLS
Fluffy in an official Girl Scout uniform. 11½". ca. 1975. ©Effan-
bee Doll Co. *(Courtesy of Harry G. Schreffler, Boy Scout and Girl Scout
Museum, Franklin, MA.)*

$50.00 – 100.00 – 125.00.

GIRL SCOUT DOLLS
**Fluffy in an official Brownie uni-
form.** 8". ca. 1975. ©Effanbee Doll Co.
*(Courtesy of Harry G. Schreffler, Boy Scout
and Girl Scout Museum, Franklin, MA.)*
$25.00 – 50.00 – 75.00.

BLUE BIRD DOLLS
Blue Bird. 24". Mfg. Unk. ca. 1940's.
*(Courtesy of Judith Radley - Nancy Ann
Doll Collector.)*
$100.00 – 150.00.

BOY SCOUT TEDDY BEARS
Boy Scout. 19". J.J. Wind Inc. 1986. *(Courtesy of Harry G. Schreffler, Boy Scout-Girl Scout Museum, Franklin, MA.)*

$50.00 ~ 75.00 ~ 125.00.

BOY SCOUT TEDDY BEARS
Cub Scout. 91". J.J. Wind Inc. 1986. *(Courtesy of Harry G. Schreffler, Boy Scout - Girl Scout Museum, Franklin, MA.)*

$50.00 ~ 75.00 ~ 125.00.

BOY SCOUT DOLLS
Felt Boy Scout. 8". Mfg. Unk. ca. 1930's. *(Courtesy of Harry G. Schreffler, Boy Scout - Girl Scout Museum, Franklin, MA.)*

$125.00 ~ 250.00.

BOY SCOUT DOLLS
English Boy Scout. 5". Mfg. Unk. England. ca. 1940. *(Courtesy of Harry G. Schreffler, Boy Scout - Girl Scout Museum, Franklin, MA.)*

$75.00 ~ 150.00 ~ 175.00.

NOTE: See the Effanbee chapter listings for additional Girl Scout dolls not pictured.

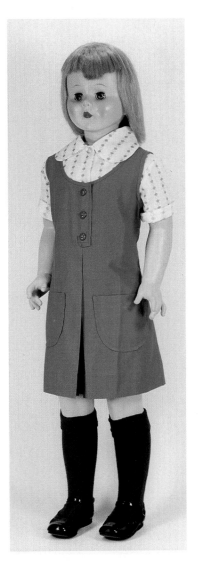

Boy Scout Dolls
Cub Scout. 40". Doll marked 40-B inside arm. Mfg. Unk. 1960's. Size 5 official Cub Scout uniform. 1970's period. *(Author's collection.)*
$25.00 ~ 50.00 ~ 75.00.

Girl Scout Dolls
Brownie. 40". Doll marked 40-B inside arm. Mfg. Unk. 1960's. Size 5 official Brownie uniform, 1985 period. *(Author's collection.)*
$25.00 ~ 50.00 ~ 75.00.

Girl Scout Dolls
Girl Scout. 40". Doll marked 40-B inside arm. Mfg. Unk. 1960's. Size 5 official Girl Scout uniform. 1985 period. *(Author's collection.)*
$25.00 ~ 50.00 ~ 75.00.

GORDY INTERNATIONAL
602 Soldier. 10". Plastic body. Articulated at wrists, shoulders, and neck. Molded on army fatigues. Mark: none. "Made in Hong Kong" on the package. Molded light brown hair. Painted blue eyes. 1977.

$10.00 – 25.00 – 30.00.

UNIFORMED TEDDY BEARS
Grenadier Guardsman. 19". Merrythough Co. of England. ca. 1985. *(Courtesy of David Grant. The Antique Stop.)*

$110.00 – 150.00 – 165.00.

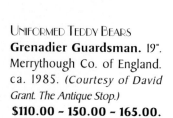

UNIFORMED TEDDY BEARS
Bobby. 19". Merrythough Co. of England. Ca. 1985. *(Courtesy of David Grant. The Antique Stop.)*

$110.00 – 150.00 – 165.00.

DOLLS NOT PICTURED

HARTLAND PLASTICS, INC.

804. Sgt. Lance O'Rourke. 8". Canadian Mounted Policeman. Plastic body. Molded on "Mountie" uniform. Articulated at shoulders. Legs bowed to fit on a horse. Removable hat. No name horse included in package. 1974.

$75.00 ~ 150.00 ~ 225.00.

804. Sgt. Preston of the Yukon. 8". Canadian Mounted Policeman. Description same as Sgt. Lance O'Rourke. The Hartland Company used the identical figures, even the same model numbers for both packages. 1974.

$75.00 ~ 150.00 ~ 225.00.

808. Gen. Robert E. Lee. 8". Plastic body. Molded on Confederate army officer's uniform. Other characteristics as Sgt. Lance O'Rourke. Gen. Lee's horse Traveler is included. 1974.

$65.00 ~ 100.00 ~ 165.00.

814. Gen. Custer. 8". Plastic body. Molded on U.S. Cavalry officer's uniform. Other characteristics same as Sgt. Lance O'Rourke. Gen. Custer's horse Bugler is included. 1974.

$65.00 ~ 100.00 ~ 165.00.

815. Gen. George Washington. 8". Plastic body. U.S. Army officer's uniform of the period is molded on. Other characteristics same as Sgt. Lance O'Rourke. Gen. Washington's horse Ajax is included. 1974.

$65.00 ~ 100.00 ~ 165.00.

PEGGY NISBET UNIFORMED DOLLS
Grenadier Guardsman. 8". #B-317. Peggy Nisbet of England. *(Courtesy of David Grant. The Antique Stop.)*
$25.00 ~ 50.00 ~ 65.00.

HASBRO INDUSTRIES

Many G.I. Joes are still found at yard sales and at flea markets. They have been played with, but they are still in very good condition. It is a good "find" if they still have their original clothing. However, in most cases they are found nude or in mismatched clothing that is unlike the original. This section is devoted to the serious collector who wishes to identify a nude G.I. Joe. The identification, classification scheme, and numbering system is based on the following criteria and rationale.

1. The year that the G.I. Joe was made.
2. The particulars of the mold mark.
3. The alphabetical listing of the hair color.
4. The original uniform G.I. Joe wore when he was "mint in box."
5. The preponderance of G.I. Joes that had the hair and eye color for the designated service even though the toy catalogs stated they were available in "Assorted hair and eye color."
6. Several succeeding years of toy catalogs that did not carry the phrase "Assorted hair and eye color."
7. The more recent toy catalogs that do state specific hair and eye color for the land, sea, and air designation.
8. The author's preference and poetic license in using the above stated criteria.

There are three generations of G.I. Joes based on their physical sizes.

1st Generation: All G.I. Joes that are 11½" tall (30 centimeters), produced from 1964 to 1976.

2nd Generation: All Super Joes that are approximately 8½" tall (22 centimeters), produced from 1976 to 1978.

3rd Generation: All G.I. Joes that are approximately 3¾" tall (9.5 centimeters), produced from 1982 to the present.

Each generation is divided into groups and each group is assigned collector's numbers according to the criteria established.

The value guide suggests a "range" for a nude G.I. Joe, in excellent condition.

1st Generation G.I. Joes

Group I – The identifying characteristic is the letters TM in the mold mark. TM stands for trademark. All have scars on the right side of their faces. Collector's numbers 1, 2, 3 & 4 were all produced at the same time in 1964. Collector's number 5 was produced early in 1965. Each have the following mold mark on the lower right-hand side of their back.

G.I. Joe TM
Copyright 1964
By Hasbro®
Patent Pending
Made in U.S.A.

HASBRO INDUSTRIES
Collector #1. Item #7500.
G.I. Joe Action Soldier.
White, black molded hair, blue eyes.
nude: $50.00 - 75.00.
$100.00 - 150.00 - 200.00.

HASBRO INDUSTRIES
Collector #2. Item #7800 **G.I. Joe Action Pilot.** White, blond molded hair, brown eyes.
nude: $50.00 - 75.00.
$150.00 - 300.00 - 400.00.

HASBRO INDUSTRIES
Collector #3. Item #7700. **G.I. Joe Action Marine.** White, brown molded hair, brown eyes.
nude: $50.00 ~ 75.00.
$100.00 ~ 275.00 ~ 375.00.

HASBRO INDUSTRIES
Collector #4. Item #7600. **G.I. Joe Action Sailor.** White, red molded hair, blue eyes.
nude: $50.00 ~ 75.00.
$100.00 ~ 250.00 ~ 325.00.

HASBRO INDUSTRIES
Collector #5. Item #7900. **G.I. Joe Action Soldier.** Black, black molded hair, brown eyes.
nude: $100.00 ~ 150.00.
$500.00 ~ 900.00 ~ 1,400.00.

HASBRO INDUSTRIES
Group II – The TM in the mold mark has been replaced with an ®. The words Patent Pending are still in the mold mark. All have scars. Collector's numbers 6, 7, 8, 9 & 10 were produced in 1965. Collector's number 11 was produced in 1966. Each have the following mold mark.

G.I. Joe ®
Copyright 1964
By Hasbro ®
Patent Pending
Made in U.S.A.

Collector #7. **G.I. Joe Action Soldier.** White, black molded hair, blue eyes. In dress uniform from "Military Police Set" #7521. Helmet from "Military Police" #7539.

nude: $45.00 – 65.00.
$100.00 – 150.00 – 200.00.

Collector #6. Item #7900. **G.I. Joe Action Soldier Negro** with box. Black, black molded hair, brown eyes.

nude: $75.00 – 100.00.
$150.00 – 250.00 – 300.00.

Collector #8. Item #7800. **G.I. Joe Action Pilot.** White, blond molded hair, brown eyes. In "Dress Uniform Set" #7803. 1965.

nude: $45.00 – 65.00.
$150.00 – 300.00 – 400.00.

Collector #9. Item #7700. **G.I. Joe Action Marine.** White, brown molded hair, brown eyes. In "Dress Parade Set" #7710. 1965.

nude: $45.00 – 65.00.
$100.00 – 275.00 – 375.00.

HASBRO INDUSTRIES
Collector #10. Item #7900. **G.I. Joe Action Sailor**. White, red molded hair, blue eyes. In "Shore Patrol Set" #7612. 1965.
nude: $45.00 – 65.00.
$100.00 – 250.00 – 325.00.

HASBRO INDUSTRIES
Collector #11. Item #8101. **G.I. Joe Japanese Imperial Soldier.** White, black molded hair, black eyes.
nude: $175.00 – 200.00.
$750.00 – 1,900.00 – 2,200.00.

HASBRO INDUSTRIES
Group III – This group was sold through the Sears and Roebuck mail order catalog as a Sears exclusive. They do not have a scar on their faces. Except for the Japanese Imperial Soldier, all have Caucasian looking faces. Any one of them may have been used for any of the five remaining "Action Soldiers of the World" and the regular action service men. The mold mark remains the same as Group II. Collector's numbers 12 through 17 were produced in 1966.

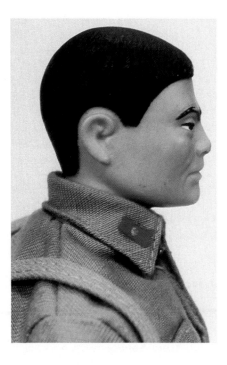

=== DOLLS NOT PICTURED ===

HASBRO INDUSTRIES
12. G.I. Joe Action Soldier, Negro. Black molded hair, brown eyes.
$35.00 – 65.00.

15. G.I. Joe Action Pilot. White, blond molded hair, brown eyes.
$35.00 – 65.00.

16. G.I. Joe Action Marine. White, brown molded hair, brown eyes.
$35.00 – 65.00.

HASBRO INDUSTRIES
Collector #13. Item #8101. **G.I. Joe Japanese Imperial Soldier.** White, black molded hair, black eyes. 1966.
nude: $150.00 – 200.00.
$700.00 – 1,800.00 – 2,300.00.

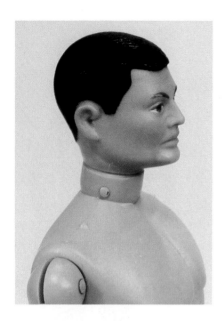

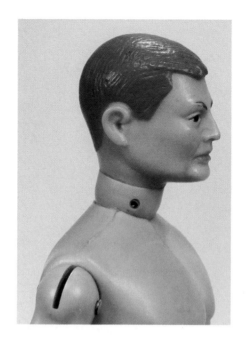

Hasbro Industries
Collector #14. Item #7500. **G.I. Joe Action Soldier,** White, black molded hair, blue eyes. 1966.

nude: $35.00 ~ 65.00.
$100.00 ~ 150.00 ~ 200.00.

Hasbro Industries
Collector #17. Item #7600. **G.I. Joe Action Sailor.** White, red molded hair, blue eyes. 1966.

nude: $35.00 ~ 65.00.
$100.00 ~ 250.00 ~ 325.00.

Hasbro Industries
Item #7536. **G.I. Joe Green Beret.** Hassenfeld Bros., Inc. 1966.

$275.00 ~ 950.00 ~ 1,600.00.

Hasbro Industries
Group IV – The mold mark has been changed. The words Patent Pending have been replaced with Pat. 3,277,602. This group of G.I. Joes does not have a scar on their faces. They are the Sears and Roebuck mail order catalog exclusives for the year 1967. Collector's numbers 18 through 27 were produced in 1967.

Collector's numbers 24 through 27 were the first talking G.I. Joes. If their programmed sound mechanism works they can be identified by the phrases they speak. If their programmed sound mechanism is mute, then the following characteristics apply to designate their military services.

═══════ Dolls Not Pictured ═══════

Hasbro Industries
18. G.I. Joe Action Soldier, Negro. Black, molded hair, brown eyes.
$25.00 ~ 65.00.

19. G.I. Joe Japanese Imperial Soldier. White, black molded hair, blue eyes.
$150.00 ~ 175.00.

20. G.I. Joe Action Soldier. White, black molded hair, blue eyes.
$25.00 ~ 65.00.

21. G.I. Joe Action Pilot. White, blond molded hair, brown eyes.
$25.00 ~ 65.00.

22. G.I. Joe Action Marine. White, brown molded hair, brown eyes.
$25.00 ~ 65.00.

23. G.I. Joe Action Sailor. White, red molded hair, blue eyes.
$25.00 ~ 65.00.

25. Talking G.I. Joe Action Pilot. White, blond molded hair, brown eyes.
$35.00 ~ 75.00.

26. Talking G.I. Joe Action Marine. White, brown molded hair, brown eyes.
$35.00 ~ 75.00.

27. Talking G.I. Joe Action Sailor. White, red molded hair, blue eyes.
$35.00 ~ 75.00.

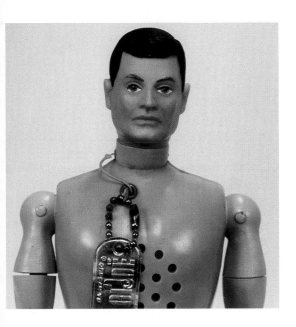

HASBRO INDUSTRIES
Collector #24. Item #7590. **Talking G.I. Joe Action Soldier.** White, black molded hair, blue eyes. 1967.
nude: $35.00 - 75.00.

HASBRO INDUSTRIES
G.I. Joe Fighting Men. German Stormtrooper. Item #8200. Hassenfeld Bros., 1967.
$225.00 - 700.00 - 1,000.00.

HASBRO INDUSTRIES
G.I. Joe Fighting Men. Russian Infantry Man. Item #8202. Hassenfeld Bros., Inc., 1967.
$250.00 - 700.00 - 1,000.00.

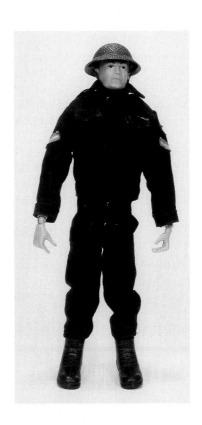

HASBRO INDUSTRIES
G.I. Joe Fighting Men. British Commando. Item #8204. Hassenfeld Bros., Inc., 1967.
$250.00 - 700.00 - 1,000.00.

Group V – This is made up of the only women in the 1st generation of G.I. Joes. It consists of two models which are distinguished from each other by the color of their hair. Collector's number 28 was made in 1967 and Collector's number 29 was made in both 1967 and 1968. Each have the same mold mark which is found in the small of their back. The mold mark is Patent Pending/ © 1967 Hasbro ®/ Made in Hong Kong.

═══════ DOLLS NOT PICTURED ═══════

HASBRO INDUSTRIES
28. G.I. Nurse Action Girl. White, brown rooted hair, green eyes.
$500.00 - 700.00.

HASBRO INDUSTRIES
Collector #29. Item #8060. **G.I. Nurse Action Girl.** White, blonde rooted hair, green eyes.

nude: **$200.00 - 700.00.**
$1,200.00 - 2,000.00 - 3,000.00.

The G.I. Joe Adventure Team was introduced in 1970. When the G.I. Joes were checked for mold marks, it was discovered that there were two different mold marks. Each G.I. Joe has one of the two mold markings. The first is the same mold mark as Group VI, and the second is:

G.I. Joe REG TM
© RD 1964
HASSENFELD BROS, INC
PATENTED 1966

The second mold mark would seem to suggest that in order to insure a good supply of adventure team G.I. Joes for retailers, all available molds were pressed into service. The above mold was in service long enough to produce many G.I. Joes with the characteristics indicated in Group VII.

Group VI – The mold mark in this group is the same as in group IV. All of the models have a scar on their right cheeks. Collector's numbers 30 through 39 were produced from 1967 through 1969.

=== DOLLS NOT PICTURED ===

HASBRO INDUSTRIES
30. G.I. Joe Japanese Imperial Soldier. White, black molded hair, black eyes.

$150.00 - 175.00.

31. G.I. Joe Action soldier, Negro. Black molded hair, brown eyes.
$25.00 - 65.00.

32. G.I. Joe Action Soldier. White, black molded hair, blue eyes.
$25.00 - 65.00.

33. G.I. Joe Action Pilot. White, blond molded hair, brown eyes.
$25.00 - 65.00.

34. G.I. Joe Action Marine. White, brown molded hair, brown eyes.
$25.00 - 65.00.

35. G.I. Joe Action Sailor. White, red molded hair, blue eyes.
$25.00 - 65.00.

36. G.I. Joe Action Soldier. White, black molded hair, blue eyes.
$35.00 - 75.00.

37. Talking G.I. Joe Action Pilot. White, blond molded hair, brown eyes.

$35.00 - 75.00.

38. Talking G.I. Joe Action Marine. White, brown molded hair, brown eyes.

$35.00 - 75.00.

39. Talking G.I. Joe Action Sailor. White, red molded hair, blue eyes.

$35.00 - 75.00.

Group VII — This group is identified by the flocked hair and beard and the following mold mark. G.I. Joe REG TM / © RD 1964 / HASSENFELD BROS. INC / PATENTED 1966. Collector's numbers 40 through 49 were produced in 1970. NOTE: None were found with Kung-Fu grip, but a G.I. Joe can easily be hybridized as the hands can be removed and replaced.

=========== DOLLS NOT PICTURED ===========

HASBRO INDUSTRIES

41. G.I. Joe Astronaut. White, blond lifelike hair, blue eyes.
$25.00 – 65.00.

44. G.I. Joe Land Adventurer. White, brown lifelike hair and beard, blue eyes.
$25.00 – 65.00.

47. Talking G.I. Joe Man of Action. White, brown lifelike hair, blue eyes.
$35.00 – 75.00.

HASBRO INDUSTRIES
Collector #40. Item #7404. **G.I. Joe Adventurer** with box. Black, black lifelike hair, brown eyes.
nude: $25.00 – 65.00.
$100.00 – 175.00 – 225.00.

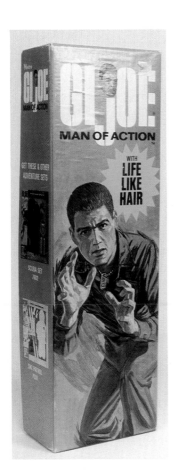

HASBRO INDUSTRIES
Collector #42. Item #7500. **G.I. Joe Man of Action.** White, brown lifelike hair, blue eyes. 1970.
nude: $25.00 – 65.00.
$75.00 – 175.00 – 225.00.

HASBRO INDUSTRIES
Collector #43. Item #7403. **G.I. Joe Air Adventurer.** White, blond lifelike hair and beard, brown eyes. 1970.

nude: $25.00 – 65.00.
$75.00 – 150.00 – 200.00.

HASBRO INDUSTRIES
Collector #45. Item #7402. **G.I. Joe Sea Adventurer.** White, red lifelike hair and beard, brown eyes.

nude: $25.00 – 65.00.
$75.00 – 175.00 – 225.00.

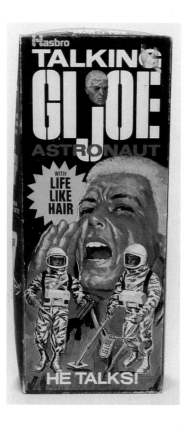

HASBRO INDUSTRIES
Collector #46. Item #7405. **Talking G.I. Joe Astronaut.** White, blond lifelike hair, brown eyes. In space suit from "Space Capsule" set #8020.

nude: $35.00 – 75.00.
$125.00 – 225.00 – 325.00.

HASBRO INDUSTRIES
Collector #48. Item #7400. **Talking G.I. Joe Adventure Team Commander.**
White, brown lifelike hair and beard, blue eyes. 1970.

nude: $35.00 ~ 75.00.
$100.00 ~ 150.00 ~ 200.00.

HASBRO INDUSTRIES
Collector #49. Item #7406.
Talking G. I. Joe Black Adventure Team Commander. Black, black lifelike hair and beard, brown eyes.
nude: $35.00 ~ 75.00.
$90.00 ~ 175.00 ~ 225.00.

HASBRO INDUSTRIES
Group VIII — The mold mark is the same as in group IV. This group is identified by their flocked hair and beards. The flocked hair and beards are called "lifelike hair." Collector's numbers 50 through 58 were produced from 1970 through 1973. Collector's number 59 was introduced in 1973.

═══════ DOLLS NOT PICTURED ═══════

HASBRO INDUSTRIES
50. G.I. Joe Adventurer. Black, lifelike hair, brown eyes.
$20.00 ~ 60.00.

51. G.I. Joe Astronaut. White, blond lifelike hair, brown eyes.
$20.00 ~ 60.00.

52. G.I. Joe Man of Action. White, brown lifelike hair, blue eyes.
$20.00 ~ 60.00.

54. G.I. Joe Land Adventurer. White, brown lifelike hair and beard, blue eyes.
$20.00 ~ 60.00.

Dolls Not Pictured

Hasbro Industries

55. G.I. Joe Sea Adventurer. White, red lifelike hair and beard, brown eyes.

$20.00 ~ 60.00.

56. Talking G.I. Joe Astronaut. White, blond lifelike hair, brown eyes.

$30.00 ~ 70.00.

57. Talking G.I. Joe Man of Action. White, brown lifelike hair, blue eyes.

$30.00 ~ 70.00.

58. Talking G.I. Joe Adventure Team Commander. White, brown lifelike hair and beard, blue eyes.

$30.00 ~ 70.00.

Hasbro Industries

Collector #53. Item #7282. **G.I. Joe Air Adventurer.** 1974. White, blond lifelike hair and beard, brown eyes.

nude: $20.00 ~ 60.00.
$50.00 ~ 150.00 ~ 175.00.

Hasbro Industries

Collector #59. Item #7291. **G.I. Joe Black Adventure Team Commander.** Black, black lifelike hair and beard, brown eyes.

nude: $30.00 ~ 70.00.
$175.00 ~ 250.00 ~ 300.00.

Group IX — The mold mark of this group is the same as group IV. This group has all the same characteristics as in group VII with the big difference being in a new pair of flexible hands that can easily grasp objects. These hands are called "Kung-Fu Grip" hands. Collector's numbers 60 through 67 were produced in 1974 and 1975.

═══ DOLLS NOT PICTURED ═══

HASBRO INDUSTRIES

61. G.I. Joe Man of Action. White, brown lifelike hair, blue eyes.
$20.00 ~ 60.00.

62. G.I. Joe Air Adventurer. White, blond lifelike hair and beard, brown eyes.
$20.00 ~ 60.00.

64. G.I. Joe Sea Adventurer. White, red lifelike hair and beard, brown eyes.
$20.00 ~ 60.00.

65. G.I. Joe Talking Black Adventure Team Commander. Black lifelike hair and beard, brown eyes.
$30.00 ~ 70.00.

66. G.I. Joe Talking Man of Action. White, brown lifelike hair, blue eyes.
$30.00 ~ 70.00.

HASBRO INDUSTRIES
Collector #60. Item #7283. **G.I. Joe Black Adventurer.** Black, black lifelike hair, brown eyes. 1975. Note: Molded on blue briefs.
nude: $20.00 ~ 60.00.
$100.00 ~ 150.00 ~ 200.00.

HASBRO INDUSTRIES
Collector #63. Item #1-7280. **G.I. Joe Land Adventurer.** White, brown lifelike hair and beard, blue eyes. 1974. Note: Muscled body. Called "muscle men" by collectors.
nude: $20.00 ~ 60.00.
$50.00 ~ 125.00 ~ 150.00.

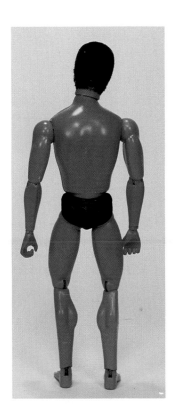

HASBRO INDUSTRIES
Collector #67. Item #7290. **G.I. Joe Talking Adventure Team Commander.** White, brown lifelike hair and beard, blue eyes. 1974.
nude: $30.00 – 70.00.
$75.00 – 150.00 – 175.00.

HASBRO INDUSTRIES
Group X — There are five models in this group with unique identifying characteristics. Collector's numbers 68 and 72 were produced in 1975 and 1976, and collector's numbers 69, 70, and 71 were produced in 1976.

HASBRO INDUSTRIES
Collector #68. Item #8025. **Mike Power, Atomic Man.** White, brown molded hair, transparent right arm and left leg.

nude: $20.00 – 50.00.
$25.00 – 75.00 – 100.00.

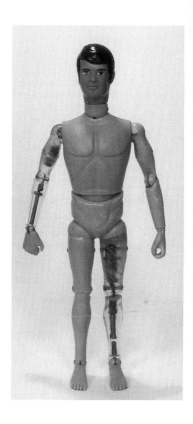

HASBRO INDUSTRIES
Collector #69. Item #8026. **Bullet Man, the Human Bullet.**
White, brown molded hair, silver metallic arms. 1976.
>**nude: $20.00 ~ 50.00.**
>**$50.00 ~ 125.00 ~ 150.00.**

HASBRO INDUSTRIES
Collector #70. Item #8050. **Intruder Comman-der.** White, brown molded hair and beard, squat heavy-set body, aluminum colored eyes, no pupils. 1976.
>**nude: $20.00 ~ 40.00.**
>**$50.00 ~ 75.00 ~ 90.00.**

HASBRO INDUSTRIES
Collector #71. Item #8051.
Intruder Warrior. White, brown molded hair, squat heavy-set body, aluminum col-ored eyes, no pupils. 1976.
>**nude: $20.00 ~ 40.00.**
>**$50.00 ~ 75.00 ~ 90.00.**

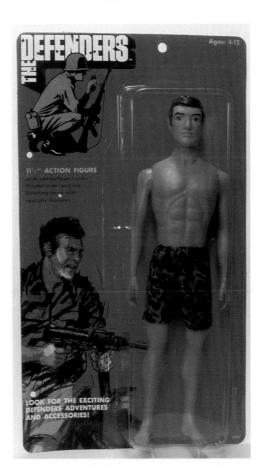

HASBRO INDUSTRIES
Collector #72. Item #9000.
The Defender. (This is not a G.I. Joe.) White, brown molded hair, brown eyes, five points of articulation. 1976.
>**nude: $15.00 ~ 25.00.**
>**$25.00 ~ 50.00 ~ 65.00.**

HASBRO INDUSTRIES

Group XI — The completely redesigned G.I. Joe makes up this group. The best identifying characteristic is the molded on blue swim trunks. Collectors call these G.I. Joes "muscle men." Collector's numbers 73 through 80 were produced in 1975. The mold mark is as follows. © 1975 Hasbro ® / PAT. PEND. PAWT. R.I.

═══════════ DOLLS NOT PICTURED ═══════════

HASBRO INDUSTRIES

73. G.I. Joe New Lifelike Black Adventurer. Black lifelike hair, brown eyes.

$20.00 – 50.00.

74. G.I. Joe New Lifelike Man of Action. White, brown lifelike hair, blue eyes.

$20.00 – 50.00.

75. G.I. Joe New Lifelike Air Adventurer. White, blond lifelike hair and beard, brown eyes.

$20.00 – 50.00.

76.G.I. Joe New Lifelike Land Adventurer. White, brown lifelike hair and beard, blue eyes.

$20.00 – 50.00.

77. G.I. Joe New Lifelike Sea Adventurer. White, red lifelike hair and beard, brown eyes.

$20.00 – 50.00.

78. G.I. Joe New Lifelike Talking Commander. Black, black lifelike hair and beard, brown eyes.

$25.00 – 55.00.

79. G.I. Joe New Lifelike Talking Commander. White, brown lifelike hair and beard, blue eyes.

$25.00 – 55.00.

80. G.I. Joe New Lifelike Talking Man of Action. White, brown lifelike hair, blue eyes.

$25.00 – 55.00.

Group XII

81. G.I. Joe Eagle Eye Commando. Black, black lifelike hair, brown eyes.

$45.00 – 75.00.

HASBRO INDUSTRIES

Group XII — This group represents the last modification of the 1st generation of G.I. Joe figures. This group is easily identified by the small lever protruding from the back of the head of G.I. Joe. Collector's numbers 81 through 83 were produced in 1976. The mold mark is © 1975 Hasbro ® / PAT. PEND. PAWT. R.I.

HASBRO INDUSTRIES

Collector #82. Item #7277. **G.I. Joe Eagle Eye Man of Action.** White, brown lifelike hair, blue eyes. 1976.

nude: $25.00 – 50.00.
$65.00 – 100.00 – 125.00.

2nd Generation G.I. Joes

Group XIII — This group is identified by their 8½" size. Individuals are identified by their specific color and body characteristics.

Hasbro Industries
Collector #83. Item #7276. **G.I. Joe Eagle Eye Land Commander.** White, brown lifelike hair and beard, blue eyes.
                        nude: $25.00 – 50.00.
                        $65.00 – 100.00 – 125.00.

Hasbro Industries
Collector #84. Item #7501. **Super Joe Commander**. White, black molded hair and beard. 1976.
                        nude: $15.00 – 20.00.
                        $25.00 – 35.00 – 50.00.

Hasbro Industries
Collector #85. Item #7502. **Super Joe Black Commander.** 1976. Black, black molded hair with a deep pointed receding hair line into the hair parting.
                        nude: $15.00 – 20.00.
                        $30.00 – 40.00 – 50.00.

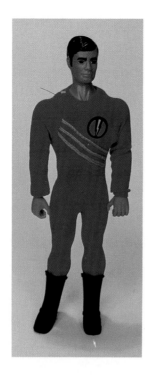

HASBRO INDUSTRIES
Collector #86. Item # 7503. **Super Joe.** 1976. White, brown molded hair.

nude: **$15.00 ~ 20.00.**
$25.00 ~ 35.00 ~ 50.00.

HASBRO INDUSTRIES
Collector #88. Item #7505. **The Shield.** 1976. Blue colored body.

nude: **$15.00 ~ 20.00.**
$25.00 ~ 30.00 ~ 40.00.

HASBRO INDUSTRIES
Collector #89. Item #7506. **Luminos.** Clear transparent body. 1976.

nude: **$15.00 ~ 20.00.**
$25.00 ~ 30.00 ~ 40.00.

HASBRO INDUSTRIES
Collector #90. Item #7508. **Darkon.** Half man, half monster. 1976.

nude: **$15.00 ~ 20.00.**
$30.00 ~ 50.00 ~ 60.00.

HASBRO INDUSTRIES

87. Super Joe. Black, black molded hair with no receding hairline into the hair parting.

$15.00 – 25.00.

91. Mageton. Red colored body, magnets imbedded in the hands and feet.

$15.00 – 25.00.

92. Mirros. Shiny metallic reflective body.

$15.00 – 25.00.

94. Phosphoton. Yellow-ivory body which glows in the dark when activated by a light source.

$15.00 – 25.00.

95. Vacutron. Orange colored body with suction cups on hands and feet.

$15.00 – 25.00.

HASBRO INDUSTRIES
Collector #93. Item #7510. **Gor, King of the Terrons.** Green reptilian pattern on the body. 1976.

nude: $15.00 – 20.00.
$25.00 – 40.00 – 50.00.

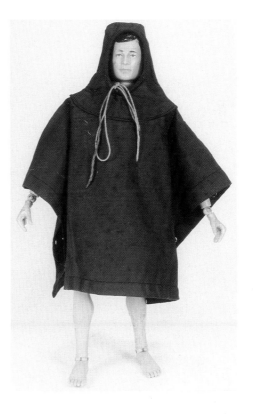

HASBRO INDUSTRIES
Poncho. Item #7519. Hassenfeld Bros., Inc. 1964.
$35.00 – 60.00 – 70.00.

HASBRO INDUSTRIES
G.I. Joe in olive drab poncho. #7519. Hassenfeld Bros., Inc. 1964.
Poncho: $35.00 – 60.00 – 70.00.

HASBRO INDUSTRIES
G.I. Joe in camoflaged poncho from "Action Marine Communication Post and Poncho Set." Hassenfeld Bros., Inc. 1964.
Poncho :
$35.00 ~ 60.00 ~ 70.00.

HASBRO INDUSTRIES
Navy Basics. #7628. Hassenfeld Bros., Ind. 1964.
$45.00 ~ 100.00 ~ 125.00.

HASBRO INDUSTRIES
Ike Jacket. #7524. Hassenfeld Bros., Inc. 1964.
$70.00 ~ 150.00 ~ 170.00.

HASBRO INDUSTRIES
Ike Pants. #7525. Hassenfeld Bros., Inc. 1964.
$65.00 ~ 150.00 ~ 170.00.

HASBRO INDUSTRIES
G.I. Joe in "Flight Suit."
#7808. Hassenfeld Bros., Inc.
1964.
   $30.00 ~ 100.00 ~ 125.00.

HASBRO INDUSTRIES
**G.I. Joe in fur parka holding
the snow sled** from "Deep
Freeze." #7623. Hasbro Ind.
   Set:
$150.00 ~ 650.00 ~ 900.00.

HASBRO INDUSTRIES
G.I. Joe Fighting Men. "French Resistance Fighter."
#8203. Hasbro Ind. 1967.

   $225.00 ~ 575.00 ~ 900.00.

HASBRO INDUSTRIES
**G.I. Joe dressed in a "French
Resistance Fighter" outfit.**
#8303. Hasbro Ind. 1967.
   $75.00 ~ 175.00 ~ 225.00.

HASBRO INDUSTRIES
G.I. Joe Fighting Men. "Australian Jungle Fighter." #8205. Hasbro Ind. 1967.
    $225.00 – 575.00 – 900.00.

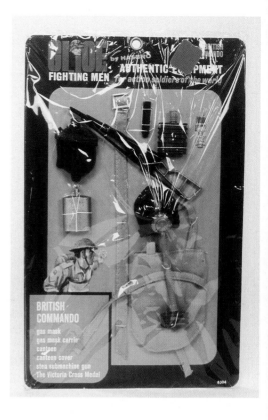

HASBRO INDUSTRIES
G.I. Joe Fighting Men. "British Commando." #8304. Hasbro Ind. 1967.
    $130.00 – 200.00 – 300.00.

HASBRO INDUSTRIES
G.I. Joe Fighting Men. "French Resistance Fighter." #8303. Hasbro Ind. 1967.
    $75.00 – 175.00 – 225.00.

HASBRO INDUSTRIES
G.I. Joe Fighting Men. "German Soldier." #8300. Hasbro Ind. 1967.
    $175.00 – 275.00 – 325.00.

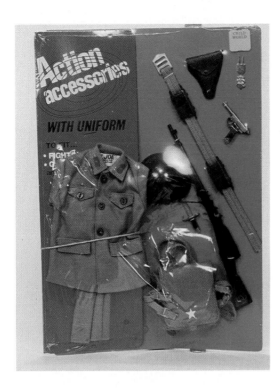

HASBRO INDUSTRIES
G.I. Joe Fighting Men. Japanese Imperial Soldier's uniform and accessories. (In close-out packaging.) #8100. Hasbro Ind. 1968.
$100.00 ~ 250.00 ~ 300.00.

HASBRO INDUSTRIES
G.I. Joe Fighting Men. German Soldier's uniform and accessories. (In close-out packaging.) #8108. Hasbro Ind. 1968.
$100.00 ~ 250.00 ~ 300.00.

HASBRO INDUSTRIES
G.I. Joe Fighting Men. Russian Soldier's uniform and accessories. (In close-out packaging.) #8108. Hasbro Ind. 1969.
$100.00 ~ 250.00 ~ 300.00.

HASBRO INDUSTRIES
G.I. Joe Fighting Men. Australian Soldier's uniform and accessories. (In close-out packaging.) #8108. Hasbro Ind. 1968.
$100.00 ~ 250.00 ~ 300.00.

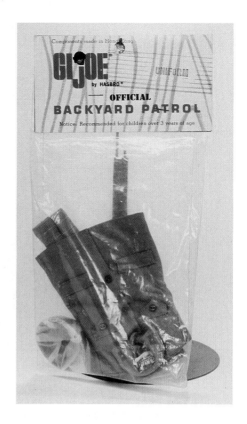

HASBRO INDUSTRIES
G.I. Joe Fighting Men. French Resistance Fighter's outfit and accessories. (In close-out packaging.) #8108. Hasbro Ind. 1968.
$100.00 ~ 200.00 ~ 250.00.

HASBRO INDUSTRIES
G.I. Joe Japanese soldier's uniform. (In close-out packaging.) Hasbro Ind. 1976.
$100.00 ~ 150.00 ~ 175.00.

HASBRO INDUSTRIES
G.I. Joe Japanese Soldier's Equipment. (In close-out packaging.) Hasbro Ind. 1976.
$150.00 ~ 300.00 ~ 325.00.

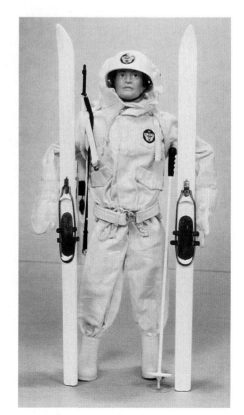

HASBRO INDUSTRIES
G.I. Joe dressed in "Ski Patrol" #7531 and "Ski Troops" #7527. Hassenfeld Bros., Inc. 1965.
$150.00 ~ 800.00 ~ 1,000.00.

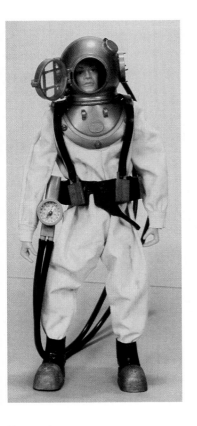

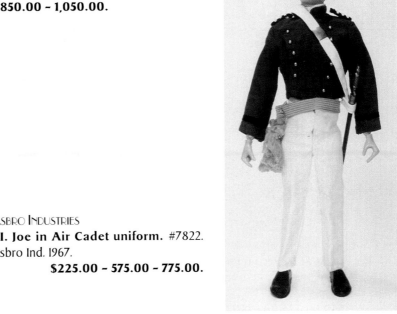

HASBRO INDUSTRIES
G.I. Joe in "Deep Sea Diver."
#7620. Hassenfeld Bros., Inc. 1965.
$150.00 ~ 1,200.00 ~ 1,400.00.

HASBRO INDUSTRIES
G.I. Joe Annapolis Cadet uniform. #7624. Hasbro Ind. 1967.
$275.00 ~ 775.00 ~ 900.00.

HASBRO INDUSTRIES
G.I. Joe in West Point Cadet uniform.
#7537. Hasbro Ind. 1967.
$250.00 ~ 850.00 ~ 1,050.00.

HASBRO INDUSTRIES
G.I. Joe in Air Cadet uniform. #7822.
Hasbro Ind. 1967.
$225.00 ~ 575.00 ~ 775.00.

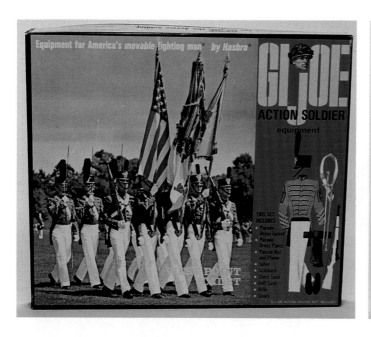

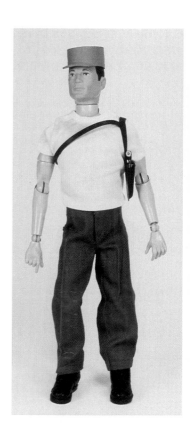

G.I. Joe West Point Cadet uniform. #7537. Hasbro Ind. 1968.

$250.00 ~ 850.00 ~ 1,050.00.

G.I. Joe Air Cadet uniform. #7822. Hasbro Ind. 1968.

$225.00 ~ 575.00 ~ 775.00.

G.I. Joe Race Car Driver uniform. #5305. Uniform sold in plain plastic bags. Hasbro Ind. ca. 1968.

$50.00 ~ 75.00 ~ 100.00.

G.I. Joe Policeman uniform. #5300. Uniform sold in plain plastic bags. Hasbro Ind. ca. 1968.

$50.00 ~ 75.00 ~ 100.00.

G.I. Joe Adventurer. #7905. Hasbro Ind. 1969.

$250.00 ~ 325.00 ~ 500.00.

HASBRO INDUSTRIES
"White Tiger Hunt." #7436. Hasbro Ind. 1970.
$100.00 ~ 175.00 ~ 200.00.

HASBRO INDUSTRIES
G.I. Joe Aquanaut. #7910. Hasbro
Ind. 1969.
 $425.00 ~ 1,300.00 ~ 1,700.00.

HASBRO INDUSTRIES
**G.I. Joe in "The Mouth of
Doom Adventure" outfit.**
#7543. Hasbro Ind. 1969.
 **Set: $100.00 ~ 175.00 ~
200.00.**

HASBRO INDUSTRIES
**G.I. Joe in "White Tiger
Hunt" outfit.** #7436. Has-
bro Ind. 1970.
 **Set: $100.00 ~ 175.00 ~
200.00.**

HASBRO INDUSTRIES
"Emergency Rescue." #7374. Hasbro Ind. 1971.
$25.00 ~ 50.00 ~ 60.00.

HASBRO INDUSTRIES
G.I. Joe in "Emergency Rescue" outfit. #7374.
Hasbro Ind. 1971.
$25.00 ~ 50.00 ~ 60.00.

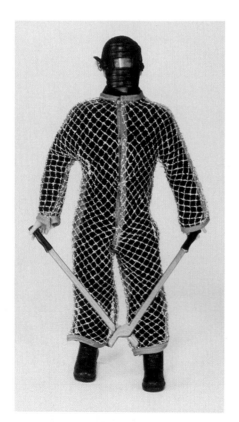

HASBRO INDUSTRIES
G.I. Joe in "High Voltage Escape."
#7342. Hasbro Ind. 1971.
$25.00 ~ 50.00 ~ 60.00.

HASBRO INDUSTRIES
"High Voltage Escape." #7342. Hasbro Ind. 1971.
$25.00 ~ 50.00 ~ 60.00.

HASBRO INDUSTRIES
G.I. Joe in "Jungle Ordeal" outfit. #7309 asst. #8203. Hasbro Ind. 1973.
$15.00 ~ 30.00 ~ 40.00.

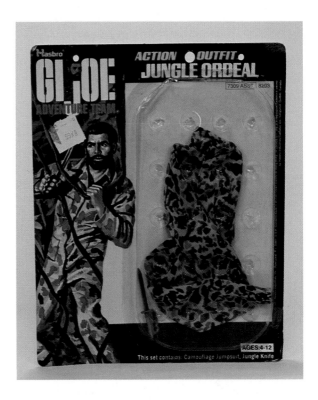

HASBRO INDUSTRIES
"Jungle Ordeal." #7309 asst. #8203. Hasbro Ind. 1973.
$15.00 ~ 30.00 ~ 40.00.

HASBRO INDUSTRIES
Japanese G.I. Joe in "Karate" outfit. #7372. Hasbro Ind. 1971.
$25.00 ~ 50.00 ~ 60.00.

HASBRO INDUSTRIES
G.I. Joe in "Black Widow Rendezvous" outfit. #7414. Hasbro Ind. 1975.
$20.00 ~ 65.00 ~ 80.00.

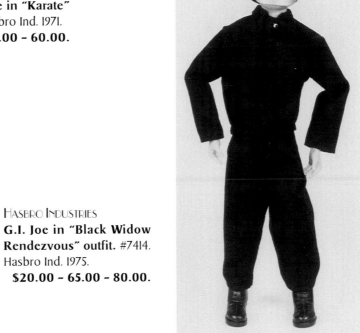

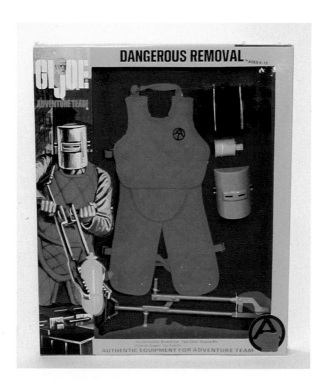

HASBRO INDUSTRIES
"Dangerous Removal." #7370. Hasbro Ind. 1971.
$35.00 – 65.00 – 75.00.

HASBRO INDUSTRIES
"Demolition." #7370. Formerly called "Dangerous Removal." Hasbro Ind. 1971.
$35.00 – 65.00 – 75.00.

HASBRO INDUSTRIES
G.I. Joe in "Jungle Survival" outfit. #7373. Hasbro Ind. 1971.
$35.00 – 75.00 – 90.00.

HASBRO INDUSTRIES
"Jungle Survival." #7373. Hasbro Ind. 1971.
$35.00 – 75.00 – 90.00.

G.I. Joe in "Secret Mission to Spy Island" outfit. Hasbro Ind. 1970.
$35.00 ~ 65.00 ~ 90.00.

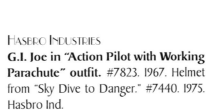

G.I. Joe in "Action Pilot with Working Parachute" outfit. #7823. 1967. Helmet from "Sky Dive to Danger." #7440. 1975. Hasbro Ind.
Outfit: $425.00 ~ 2,200.00 ~ 2,300.00.
Helmet: $25.00 ~ 65.00 ~ 75.00.

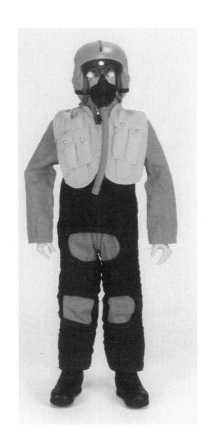

G.I. Joe in "Copter Rescue" outfit. #7308-3. Hasbro Ind. 1973.
$15.00 ~ 30.00 ~ 40.00.

G.I. Joe in "Danger Climb" outfit. #7309-2. Hasbro Ind. 1973.
$15.00 ~ 30.00 ~ 40.00.

"Mine Shaft Break Out." #7338 asst. #7331. Hasbro Ind. 1975.
$35.00 ~ 45.00 ~ 60.00.

HASBRO INDUSTRIES
"Jettison to Safety." #7338 asst. #7332. Hasbro Ind. 1975.
$35.00 ~ 45.00 ~ 60.00.

HASBRO INDUSTRIES
"Photo Recon." #7308. asst. #8201. Hasbro Ind. 1973.
$15.00 ~ 30.00 ~ 40.00.

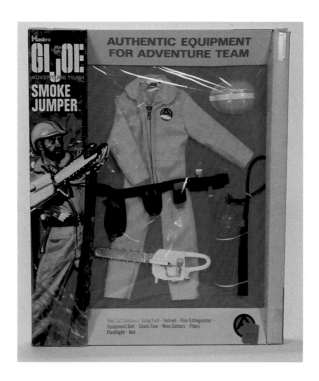

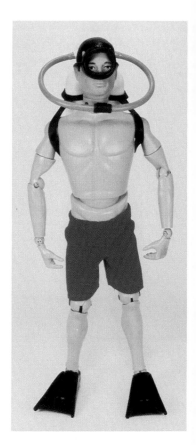

HASBRO INDUSTRIES
G.I. Joe in "Diver's Distress." #7328-6. Hasbro Ind. 1975.
$25.00 ~ 45.00 ~ 60.00.

HASBRO INDUSTRIES
"Smoke Jumper." #7378 asst. #7371. Hasbro Ind. 1971.
$35.00 ~ 75.00 ~ 90.00.

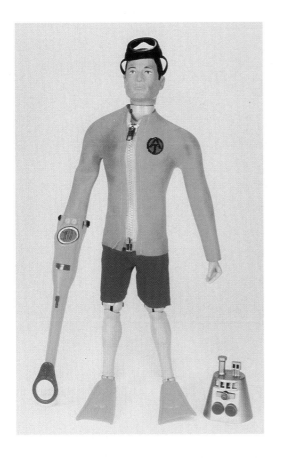

HASBRO INDUSTRIES
G.I. Joe in "Hidden Trea-sure" outfit. #7308-I. Has-bro Ind. 1973.
$15.00 ~ 30.00 ~ 40.00.

HASBRO INDUSTRIES
G.I. Joe in "Missile Recovery." #7348. Hasbro Ind. 1971.
$20.00 ~ 30.00 ~ 40.00.

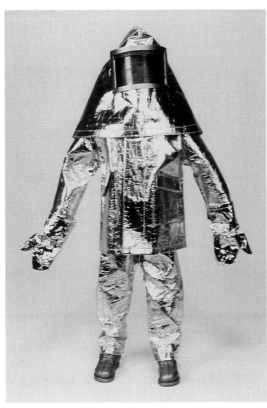

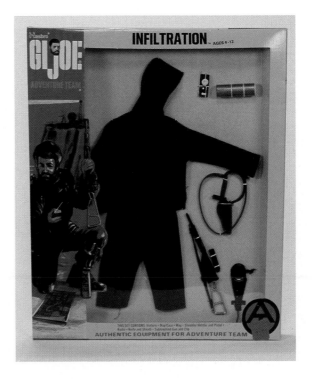

HASBRO INDUSTRIES
G.I. Joe in "Crash Crew" suit. #7820. Hasbro Ind. 1966.

$100.00 ~ 400.00 ~ 450.00.

HASBRO INDUSTRIES
"Infiltration." #7378 asst. Hasbro Ind. 1974.
$20.00 ~ 50.00 ~ 65.00.

Hasbro Industries
"Raging River Dam Up." #7330 asst. Hasbro Ind. 1975.
$30.00 ~ 45.00 ~ 60.00.

Hasbro Industries
"Danger Ray Detection." #7333 asst. #7339. Hasbro Ind. 1975.
$30.00 ~ 45.00 ~ 60.00.

Hasbro Industries
"Night Surveillance." #7339 asst. #7335. Hasbro Ind. 1975.
$30.00 ~ 45.00 ~ 60.00.

Hasbro Industries
"Secret Mission." #7309 asst. #8204. Hasbro Ind. 1973.
$15.00 ~ 30.00 ~ 40.00.

Hasbro Industries
G.I. Joe in "Secret Mission" outfit. #7309 asst. #8204. Hasbro Ind. 1973.
$15.00 ~ 30.00 ~ 40.00.

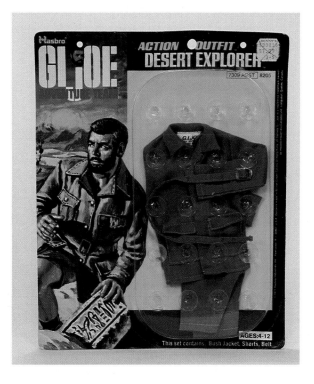

Hasbro Industries
"Desert Explorer." #7309 asst. #8205. Hasbro Ind. 1973.
$15.00 ~ 30.00 ~ 40.00.

Hasbro Industries
G.I. Joe in "Desert Explorer" outfit.
#7309 asst. #8205. Hasbro Ind. 1973.
$15.00 ~ 30.00 ~ 40.00.

Hasbro Industries
G.I. Joe in "Dangerous Mission" outfit. #7308-5. Hasbro Ind. 1973.
$15.00 ~ 30.00 ~ 40.00.

HASBRO INDUSTRIES
"Dangerous Mission." #7308-5. Hasbro Ind. 1973.
$15.00 – 30.00 – 40.00.

HASBRO INDUSTRIES
G.I. Joe in "Radiation Detector" outfit.
#7341. Hasbro Ind.
$25.00 – 50.00 – 60.00.

HASBRO INDUSTRIES
G.I. Joe in "Secret Agent"
outfit. #7375. Hasbro Ind.
1971.
$40.00 – 75.00 – 90.00.

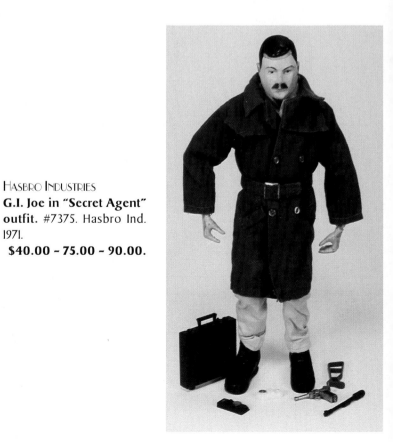

HASBRO INDUSTRIES
"Radiation Detection." #7341. Hasbro Ind. 1971.
$25.00 – 50.00 – 60.00.

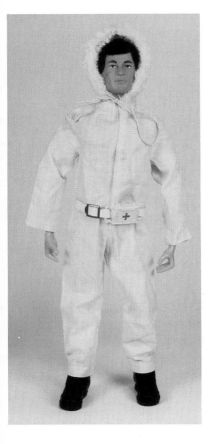

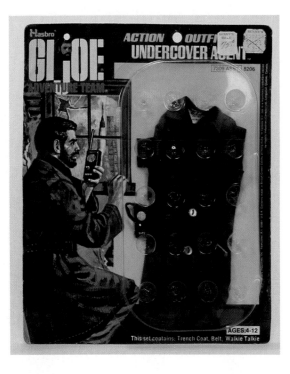

HASBRO INDUSTRIES
"Undercover Agent." #7309. asst #8206. Hasbro Ind. 1973.

$15.00 ~ 30.00 ~ 40.00.

HASBRO INDUSTRIES
G.I. Joe in "Winter Rescue" outfit.
#7309-4. Hasbro Ind. 1973.
$15.00 ~ 30.00 ~ 40.00.

HASBRO INDUSTRIES
G.I. Joe in "Undercover Agent"
outfit. #7309-6. Note and compare
the trench coat with Secret Agent.
Hasbro Ind. 1973.
$15.00 ~ 30.00 ~ 40.00.

HASBRO INDUSTRIES
G.I. Joe in "Fight for Survival
outfit. #7308 asst. Hasbro Ind. 1973.
$15.00 ~ 30.00 ~ 40.00.

HASBRO INDUSTRIES
G.I. Joe in "Magnum Power" outfit.
#7348 asst. Hasbro Ind. 1976.
$20.00 ~ 45.00 ~ 55.00.

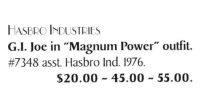

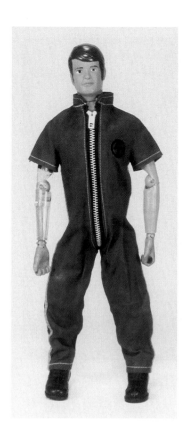

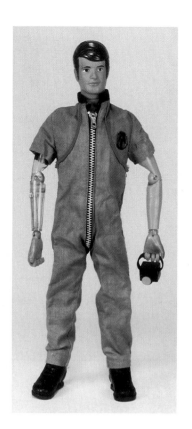

Hasbro Industries
Atomic Man, Mike Power in "Fangs of the Cobra" outfit. #8028 asst. Hasbro Ind. 1975.
$20.00 ~ 40.00 ~ 50.00.

Hasbro Industries
Atomic Man, Mike Power in "Race for Recovery" outfit. #8028 asst. Hasbro Ind. 1975.
$20.00 ~ 40.00 ~ 50.00.

Hasbro Industries
"Hidden Treasure." #7308 asst. #7300. Hasbro Ind. 1973.
$15.00 ~ 30.00 ~ 40.00.

Hasbro Industries
"Fight for Survival." #7308 asst. #7301. Hasbro Ind. 1973.
$15.00 ~ 30.00 ~ 40.00.

Hasbro Industries
"Secret Rendezvous." #7308 asst. #7303. Hasbro Ind. 1973.
$15.00 ~ 30.00 ~ 40.00.

HASBRO INDUSTRIES
"Desert Survival." #7308 asst. #7305. Hasbro Ind. 1973.
$15.00 ~ 30.00 ~ 40.00.

HASBRO INDUSTRIES
The Defenders: "Counter Attack." #4-9028. Hasbro Ind. 1975.
$10.00 ~ 25.00 ~ 30.00.

HASBRO INDUSTRIES
The Defenders: "Sniper Patrol." #3-9028. Hasbro Ind. 1975.
$10.00 ~ 25.00 ~ 30.00.

HASBRO INDUSTRIES
The Defenders: "Foward Observer." #5-9028. Hasbro Ind. 1975.
$10.00 ~ 25.00 ~ 30.00.

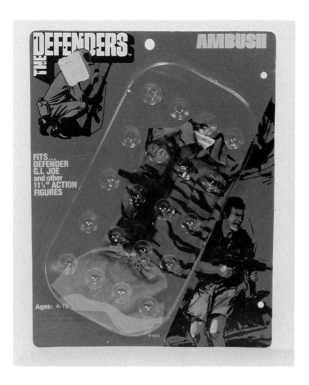

HASBRO INDUSTRIES
The Defenders: "Ambush." #6-9028. Hasbro Ind. 1975.
$10.00 ~ 25.00 ~ 30.00.

HASBRO INDUSTRIES
"Fantastic Freefall." #7423. Hasbro Ind. 1970.
$100.00 ~ 200.00 ~ 225.00.

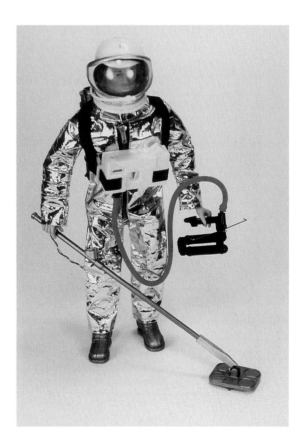

HASBRO INDUSTRIES
G.I. Joe in "The Hidden Missile Discovery Adventure" outfit. #7952. Hasbro Ind. 1969.
$75.00 ~ 175.00 ~ 225.00.

HASBRO INDUSTRIES
G.I. Joe in light blue "Deck Commander" outfit. #7621. Hassenfeld Bros., Inc. 1966.
$150.00 ~ 475.00 ~ 575.00.

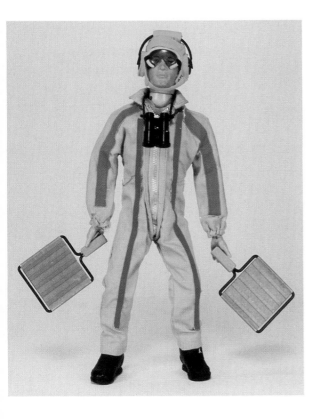

HASBRO INDUSTRIES
G.I. Joe in khaki "Deck Commander" outfit. #7621.
Hassenfeld Bros., Inc. 1966.

$125.00 – 450.00 – 575.00.

HASBRO INDUSTRIES
G.I. Joe in red and blue "Life Guard" uniform. Palitoy Co. England 1968.
(Palitoy has a licence from Hasbro to produce accessories for G.I. Joe.)

$750.00 – 1,500.00 – 2,000.00.

HASBRO INDUSTRIES
G.I. Joe Action Men. Mountie Gift set. No catalog number on box. Hasbro of Canada. 1968.

$350.00 – 1,500.00 – 2,000.00.

HASBRO INDUSTRIES
G.I. Joe "Canadian Mountie" uniform. #7389. Hasbro of
Canada. 1968.

$150.00 – 500.00 – 900.00.

69

HASBRO INDUSTRIES
"Grenadier Guards." #34302. Palitoy Co., England.
1968.

$25.00 ~ 75.00 ~ 100.00.

HASBRO INDUSTRIES
"Parachute Regiment." #34301. Palitoy Co., England. 1968.

$25.00 ~ 75.00 ~ 100.00.

HASBRO INDUSTRIES
**Action Man. "French
Great Coat."** #34279.
Palitoy Co. 1970.
**$25.00 ~ 35.00 ~
40.00.**

HASBRO INDUSTRIES
Action Man, "British Infantryman." #34317.
Palitoy Co. 1968.

$25.00 ~ 60.00 ~ 75.00.

HORSMAN DOLLS INC.
Police Women. 9". "Angie Dickinson." Plastic body. Fully articulated. Blonde rooted hair. Painted brown eyes. Mark on head: Horsman Dolls inc. / u / I GFT / 19©76.

$10.00 – 25.00 – 35.00.

IDEAL TOY CORPORATION
Captain Action. 11½". Plastic body. Articulated at the ankles, knees, hips, waist, shoulders, elbows, wrists, and neck. Black molded hair. Painted black eyes. Mark on head: © 1966 Ideal M-93. Mark on back: © 1966 / Ideal Toy Corp / 3. 1966.

$100.00 – 250.00 – 300.00.

IDEAL TOY CORPORATION
Spider Man disguise. Ideal Toy Corp. Captain Action accessory. 1966.
$100.00 – 200.00 – 250.00.

IDEAL TOY CORPORATION
Captain America disguise. Ideal Toy Corp. Captain Action accessory. 1966.
$100.00 – 200.00 – 250.00.

IDEAL TOY CORPORATION
Back of accessory package, 1966.

═══════════ DOLLS NOT PICTURED ═══════════

IDEAL TOY CORPORATION
Liberty Boy. 12". Composition body. Articulated at hips, shoulders, and neck. Molded on khaki army uniform, leggings, and boots. Blond molded hair. Painted blue eyes. Right arm bent so he can salute. Mark on back: Ideal in a diamond. 1918.
$150.00 – 250.00 – 300.00.

Soldier Boy or Flexy Soldier. 13". Composition head and hands. Wire arms and legs. Wooden feet. Light brown molded hair. Painted blue eyes. Mark on back: U.S.A. 13. 1942.
$100.00 – 150.00 – 175.00.

Sailor Boy or Flexy Sailor. 13". In sailor uniform. Description same as for Soldier Boy.
$100.00 – 150.00 – 175.00.

Miss Curity. 14¼". Hard plastic body. Articulated at hips, shoulders, and neck. Blonde glued on wig. Blue sleep eyes. Mark on head: P-90 / Ideal Doll, Made in U.S.A. Original outfit: white nurse's uniform, white nurse's cap with the words "Miss Curity." 1953.
$150.00 – 200.00 – 250.00.

Sergeant Fury. 11½". Superhero army costume for Capt. Action: face mask, olive drab helmet, green camouflage army fatigues, pistol belt with pistol and holster, boots, handie talkie, machine gun. 1966.
$100.00 – 250.00 – 300.00.

Steve Canyon. 11½". Superhero costume for Captain Action: face mask, helmet with oxygen mask, garrison cap with 50 mission crush, paratrooper uniform, parachute pack, pistol belt with 45 caliber pistol and holster, knife, boots. 1966.
$100.00 – 200.00 – 250.00.

Flash Gordon. 11½". Superhero space suit costume for Captain Action: face mask, silver space suit, space helmet, pistol belt with ray gun and holster, silver space boots. 1966.
$100.00 – 200.00 – 250.00.

Buck Rogers. 11½". Superhero space suit costume for Captain Action: face mask, blue space helmet, red vinyl dickey, silver space suit, black gloves, space boots, blue and yellow rocket jet pack, spacelight, canteen. 1966.
$100.00 – 200.00 – 250.00.

DOLLS NOT PICTURED

IDEAL TOY CORPORATION

Sailor (Whistler). 14½". In a white sailor suit and hat. Composition head and arms. Stuffed cloth body. Cloth covered coil springs formed legs. Blond molded hair. Right-looking painted blue eyes. Mouth opened forming an "O." 1930's.
$50.00 ~ 100.00 ~ 125.00.

Tammy. 12". Plastic body. Vinyl head. Articulated at hips, shoulders, and neck. Blonde rooted hair. Painted right-looking blue eyes. Mark on head: © Ideal Toy Corp / BS - 12. Mark on back: © Ideal Toy Corp / BS - 12. 1962.
$15.00 ~ 50.00 ~ 65.00.

IDEAL TOY CORPORATION

Action Boy Spaceman. 9". Plastic body. Vinyl head. Articulated at ankles, knees, hips, waist, shoulders, elbows, wrists, and neck. Brown molded hair. Painted brown eyes. Mark on head: © 1966 / Ideal Toy Corp. Mark on back: © 1967 / Ideal Toy Corp. 1967.
$200.00 ~ 300.00 ~ 350.00.

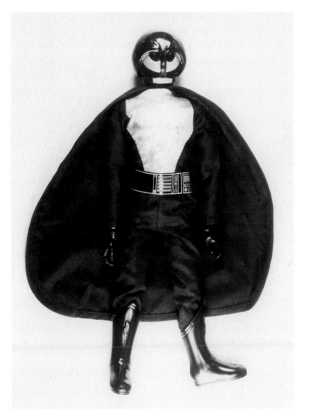

IDEAL TOY CORPORATION

4603~7. Knight of Darkness. 11½". All plastic body. (The same mold as for "Captain Action" and Dr. Evil.") Molded on helmeted head. Articulated at ankles, knees, hips, waist, shoulders, elbows, wrists, and neck. Body all black. Mark on head: © 1977 / ideal / MKP. M-285. Mark on shoulder blades: Hong Kong. 1977.
$20.00 ~ 75.00 ~ 100.00.

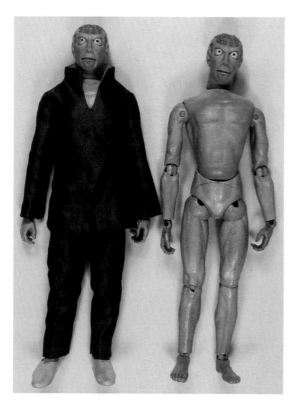  

IDEAL TOY CORPORATION
Doctor Evil in space-type lab uniform, 1988. 11½". Light blue plastic body. Articulation same as Captain Action. Top of skull missing with the brain showing. Painted blood-shot eyes. Mark on head: ©1968 Ideal H-118. Mark on back: ©1966 / Ideal Toy Corp / ©. 1968.
$150.00 – 300.00 – 350.00.

IDEAL TOY CORPORATION
Tammy, nurse. A white nurse's uniform dress and a white nurse's cap. Dress tag: Tammy T. M. / Ideal Japan. 1965.
$10.00 – 50.00 – 65.00.

IDEAL TOY CORPORATION
Tammy, candy striper. A red and white candy stripe jumper-style dress, white blouse, and a red and white candy stripe nurse's style cap. Outside dress tag: Tammy. 1965.
$10.00 – 50.00 – 65.00

JOLLY TOY COMPANY
Kaysam Red Cross Nurse. 15". Adult plastic body and legs. Vinyl head and arms. Articulated at hips, shoulders, and neck. Brown rooted hair. Blue sleep eyes. High heel feet. Mark on head: Kaysam/ 1961. Mark on lower body: 53 15/ 19©61 / Kaysam. 1961.

$35.00 – 50.00.

KENDALL COMPANY
Miss Curity Nurse. 7". Miss Curity in white nurse's uniform. Hard plastic body. Articulated only at the shoulders. Glued on blonde wig. Blue sleep eyes. Painted on white stockings. Molded on white shoes. Unifom made out of vinyl sheeting. ca. 1953.

$10.00 – 25.00 – 30.00.

KRESGE COMPANY

The Adventurer. 11½". Plastic body. Articulated. Brown molded hair. Painted brown eyes. Mark on top of back: Hong Kong. Original outfit: green camouflaged fatigues. ca. 1972.

$10.00 ~ 25.00 ~ 30.00.

KRESGE COMPANY

All Pro Sportman. 11½". Description same as the Adventurer except now packaged in a yellow sweatsuit with a red stripe along the side of the pants. ca. 1975. The dolls and packaging suggest the change over from a militay focus to sports and civilian activities.

$10.00 ~ 25.00 ~ 30.00.

KRESGE COMPANY

The Kresge Company produced the following military uniforms for the Adventurer and any other 11½" action figure. There are no names for the uniforms on the packages nor is there a model number.

═══════ DOLLS NOT PICTURED ═══════

KRESGE COMPANY

Army M.P. Package includes: white helmet, khaki jacket and pants, white belt, M.P. arm band, billy club, black low quarter shoes. 1972.

$8.00 ~ 25.00 ~ 30.00.

Naval Officer. Package includes: white garrison cap, blue dress jacket with gold stripe around the collar and two gold stripes on the lower end of the sleeve, white pants with red stripe on the side, black low quarter shoes. 1972.

$8.00 ~ 25.00 ~ 30.00.

Sailor. Package includes: white sailor hat, traditional sailor shirt with square collar, blue sailor pants, black ankle boots. 1972.

$8.00 ~ 25.00 ~ 30.00.

Ski Trooper. Package includes: white hooded parka, white pants, white ankle boots, white skis and ski poles. 1972.

$8.00 ~ 25.00 ~ 30.00.

Soldier. Package includes: green camouflaged jacket and pants, low quarter shoes. 1972.

$8.00 ~ 25.00 ~ 30.00.

KRESGE COMPANY
Arctic Explorer. Package includes: red fur-trimmed hooded parka, tan pants, white ankle boots. 1972.

$8.00 ~ 25.00 ~ 30.00.

LARAMI CORP.
8044-0 Nurse Nancy. 11½". Plastic adult body. Vinyl head. Articulated at hips, shoulders, and neck. Brown rooted hair. Painted right-looking blue eyes. Mark on back: Made in / Hong Kong. Dress tag: Made in / Hong Kong. 1970's.

$10.00 ~ 20.00 ~ 25.00.

L. I. C. COMPANY

6673. Dr. Ben of TV Fame. 11½" Thin plastic body and head. Articulated at hips, shoulders, and neck. Light brown molded hair. Painted blue eyes. Mark in small of back: Made in Hong Kong. Doctor's tunic tag: Made in Hong Kong. ca. 1965.

$10.00 ~ 25.00 ~ 30.00.

L. J. N. TOYS LTD.

#4500 "V" Enemy Visitor. 11½". Plastic body. Vinyl head. Has a molded on reptilian face which can be hidden by a human face mask (which is included in the package). The snake-like tongue is activated by a button on the back. Articulated at knees, hips, waist, shoulders, elbows, and neck. Mark: 1984/Warner Bros./ L.J.N. Toys Ltd. 1984.

$10.00 ~ 35.00 ~ 40.00.

=========== DOLLS NOT PICTURED ===========

L. J. N. TOYS LTD.

Mister Double Action. 11½". Plastic body. Articulated at ankles, knees, hips, waist, shoulders, elbows, wrists, and neck. Black molded hair and beard. Painted black eyes. 1973.

$10.00 ~ 25.00 ~ 30.00.

4444. Navy Sentry. Package includes: white sailor hat, white shirt with square collar, white pants, black low quarter shoes, white billy club (traditional navy uniform). 1973.

$8.00 ~ 25.00 ~ 30.00.

4444. Military Police. Package includes: white navy hat, khaki jacket and pants, black low quarter shoes, M.P. arm band, pistol belt with pistol and holster, billy club. 1973.

$8.00 ~ 25.00 ~ 30.00.

4444. Deep Sea Rescue. Package includes: traditional white sailor shirt and pants, orange cloth "Mae West" vest, orange vinyl inflatable raft marked U.S.N. 1973.

$8.00 ~ 25.00 ~ 30.00.

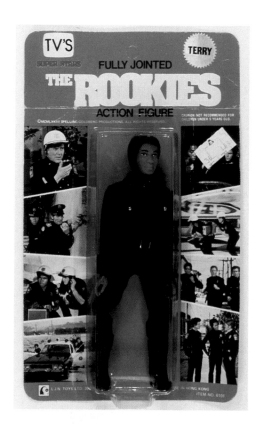

L.J.N. TOYS   *THE ROOKIES*
Willie Policeman. 7½". Plastic body with white molded on briefs.
Articulated at ankles, knees, hips, waist, elbows, wrists, shoulders,
and neck. Black molded hair. Painted blue eyes. Mark on back:
[symbol] / L. J. N. Toy Ltd. / Hong Kong / All Rights reserved. 1973.
                              $8.00 ~ 25.00 ~ 30.00.

L.J.N. TOYS   *THE ROOKIES*
Terry Policeman. 7½" Description same as Willie except
for black molded hair and painted brown eyes. 1973.
                              $8.00 ~ 25.00 ~ 30.00.

L.J.N. TOYS   *THE ROOKIES*
Chris Policeman. 7½".
Description same as Willie
except for blond molded hair
and painted blue eyes. 1973.
   $8.00 ~ 25.00 ~ 30.00.

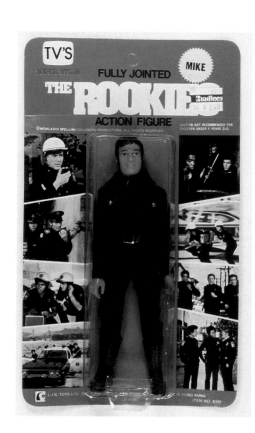

L.J.N. TOYS   *THE ROOKIES*
Mike Policeman. 7½".
Description same as Willie
except for face, black molded
hair, and painted blue eyes. 1973.
   $10.00 ~ 25.00 ~ 30.00.

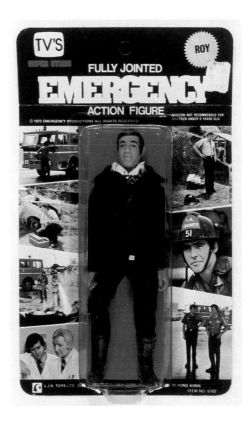

L.J.N. Toys *THE ROOKIES*
Lt. Riker Policeman. 7½". Description same as Willie except for face, black molded hair, and painted brown eyes. 1975.
$10.00 ~ 30.00 ~ 35.00.

L. J. N. Toys *EMERGENCY*
Roy Emergency Medical Team. 7½". Description same as the Rookies except face, black molded hair, and painted brown eyes. 1974.
$8.00 ~ 25.00 ~ 30.00.

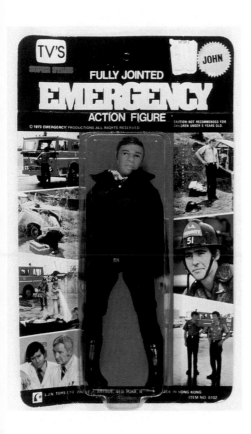

L. J. N. Toys *S.W.A.T.*
McCabe S.W.A.T. Policeman. 7½". Description same as the Rookies except for face, black molded hair, and painted brown eyes. 1975.
$8.00 ~ 25.00 ~ 30.00.

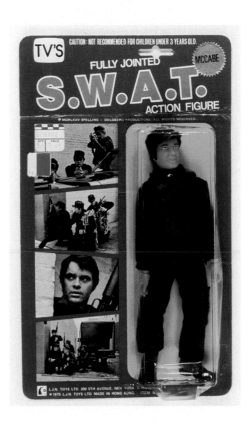

L. J. N. Toys *EMERGENCY*
John E.M.T. 7½". Description same as Roy except for face, brown molded hair, and painted brown eyes. 1974.
$8.00 ~ 25.00 ~ 30.00.

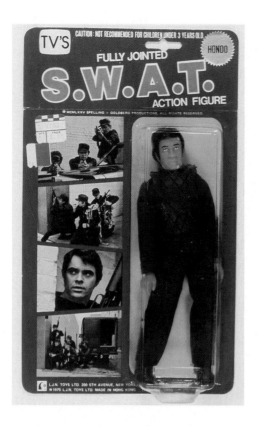

L. J. N. Toys   *S.W.A.T.*
Hondo S.W.A.T. Policeman.
7½". Description same as Street except for face, black molded hair, and painted blue eyes. 1975.
$8.00 – 25.00 – 30.00.

L. J. N. Toys   *S.W.A.T.*
Deacon S.W.A.T. Policeman.
7½" Description same as Street except for face, black molded hair, and painted brown eyes. 1975.
$8.00 – 25.00 – 30.00.

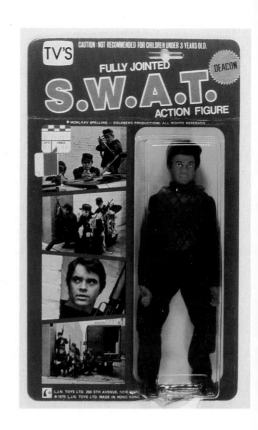

L. J. N. Toys   *S.W.A.T.*
Luca S.W.A.T. Policeman.
7½". Description same as Street except for face, blond molded hair, painted blue eyes, hands now can move up and down as well as turn at the wrist. Foot now moves up and down at the ankle, but does not turn. (All the previous dolls in the L.J.N. toy series mentioned have a ball and socket at the ankle which permits turning movement as well as up and down movement of the foot.) Distributed by F. W. Woolworth Co., N.Y. 10007. Item #6850. 1976.
$10.00 – 30.00 – 35.00.

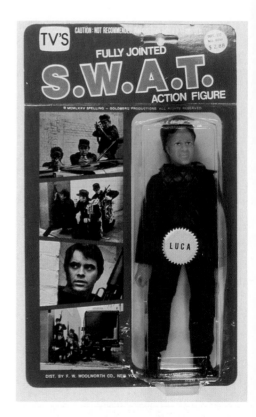

L. J. N. Toys   *S.W.A.T.*
Street S.W.A.T. Policeman. 7½". Description same as Street except for face, black molded hair, and painted blue eyes. 1975.
$8.00 – 25.00 – 30.00.

L. J. N. Toys *Police Girl*

Forest Ranger. 9". Plastic body. Articulated at hips, waist, shoulders, and neck. Rooted blond hair. Painted blue eyes. Mark on head: LJN / © 1974. Mark on back: Hong Kong. 1974.

$10.00 ~ 30.00 ~ 35.00.

L. J. N. Toys *Police Girl*

Police Girl. 9". Description same as Forest Ranger. 1974.

$10.00 ~ 30.00 ~ 35.00.

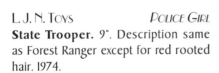

L. J. N. Toys *Police Girl*

State Trooper. 9". Description same as Forest Ranger except for red rooted hair. 1974.

$10.00 ~ 30.00 ~ 35.00.

L. J. N. TOYS   *POLICE GIRL*

Police Nurse. Black. 9". Description same as Forest Ranger except black rooted hair and painted brown eyes. 1974.

$10.00 – 30.00 – 35.00.

L. J. N. TOYS

4700. Mister Action. 11½". Plastic body. Articulated at hips, waist, shoulders, and neck. Dark brown molded hair. Painted blue eyes. Mark on body: Hong Kong. 1973.

$10.00 – 25.00 – 30.00.

L. J. N. TOYS

4700. Mister Action. 11½". Description same as previous Mister Action except for dark brown eyes and beard. 1973.

$10.00 – 25.00 – 30.00.

The L.J.N. Toys Ltd. company produced the following uniforms to fit its Mister Action as well as G.I. Joe, Fighting Yank, and other action figures. Its earlier packages have the title "Men of Action" and the model #4444. Its later packages are titled "Action Outfits" and have model #4600.

L. J. N. Toys

4444 & 4600. Marine Honor Guard. Package includes: white garrison cap, dress blue marine jacket, dress blue marine pants with red stripe on the side, black low quarter shoes, white U.S. M-I rifle with black sling. 1973.

$8.00 ~ 25.00 ~ 30.00.

L. J. N. Toys

4444 & 4600. Night Patrol. Package includes: black cloth hat, black pull-over sweater, black pants, black low quarter shoes, U.S. M-I carbine with a black sling. 1973.

$8.00 ~ 25.00 ~ 30.00.

L. J. N. Toys

4444 & 4600. Underwater Demolition. Package includes: black jumpsuit-style scuba suit, black snorkel, black face mask, and black swim fins. 1973.

$8.00 ~ 25.00 ~ 30.00.

L. J. N. Toys
4444. Jungle Guerilla. Package includes: green fatigue cap, green camouflage fatigue jacket and pants, black ankle shoes, U.S. M-I Carbine with black sling. 1973.

$8.00 ~ 25.00 ~ 30.00.

L. J. N. Toys
4600. Motorcyclist. L.J.N. Toys Ltd. 1973.

$8.00 ~ 25.00 ~ 30.00.

L. J. N. Toys
4600. Olympian. L.J.N. Toys LTD. 1973.

$8.00 ~ 25.00 ~ 30.00.

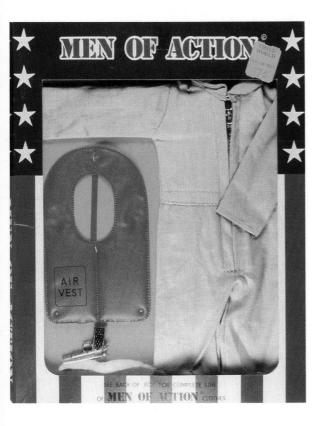

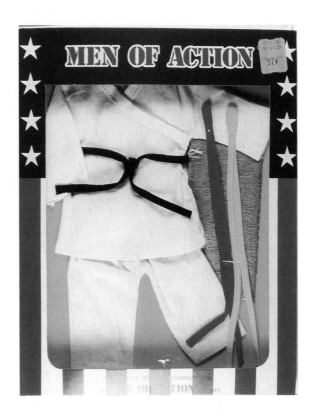

L. J. N. Toys
4444. Carrier Pilot. Package includes: light gray flight jumpsuit, orange vinyl "Mae West" vest marked: Air Vest, 45. caliber pistol.

$8.00 ~ 25.00 ~ 30.00.

L. J. N. Toys
4444 & 4600. Karate Defense. Package includes: white karate tunic and pants, black belt. 1973.

$8.00 ~ 25.00 ~ 30.00.

L. J. N. Toys
4444. Doctor. Package includes: long white coat, white pants, white low quarter shoes, red cross arm band, first aid kit. 1973.

$8.00 ~ 25.00 ~ 30.00.

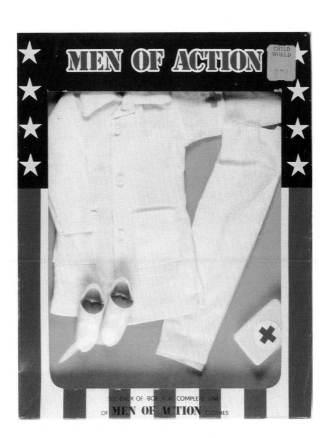

L. J. N. Toys
4600. Navy Sentry. Package includes: (traditional navy uniform), white sailor hat, blue shirt with square collar, blue pants, black low quarter shoes, billy club. 1973.

$8.00 – 25.00 – 30.00.

L. J. N. Toys
Back of Action Outfits accessory packages. #4600. L.J.N. Toys LTD. 1973.

L. J. N. Toys
4444. Grand Prix. L.J.N. Toys LTD. 1973 Orange and blue STP coveralls with black shoes.
$8.00 – 25.00 – 30.00.

L. J. N. TOYS
Back of Men of Action accessory packages.
#4444. L.J.N. Toys LTD. 1973.

MADISON LTD.
Paratrooper. Package includes: orange jumpsuit, white helmet, black ankle boots. 1980's.
$5.00 ~ 10.00 ~ 15.00.

Navy Seal. Package includes: black SCUBA-like suit, gray air tanks, snorkel, face mask, and swim fins. 1980's.
$5.00 ~ 10.00 ~ 15.00.

U.S. Marine. Package includes: traditional marine uniform of white garrison cap, blue dress jacket, blue dress pants with red stripe, white belt, black ankle shoes. 1980's.
$5.00 ~ 10.00 ~ 15.00.

Soldier. Package includes: army combat uniform of green helmet, green camouflage fatigues, pistol belt, rifle. 1980's.
$5.00 ~ 10.00 ~ 15.00.

LOVELY DOLL COMPANY
U.S. Marine. 7". Hard plastic body. Articulated at shoulders and neck. Brown molded hair. Blue sleep eyes. Painted molded on shoes. Bows on shoes. Original outfit: marine uniform of the period. ca. 1954.
$10.00 ~ 25.00 ~ 30.00.

U.S. Army. 7". Description same as U.S. Marine wearing a U.S. Army uniform of the period. ca. 1954.
$10.00 ~ 25.00 ~ 30.00.

U.S. Air Corps. 7". Description same as U.S. Marine except wearing a U.S. Air Corps uniform of the period. ca. 1954.
$10.00 ~ 25.00 ~ 30.00.

U.S. Navy. 7". Description same as U.S. Marine except wearing a U.S. Navy uniform of the period. ca. 1954.
$10.00 ~ 25.00 ~ 30.00.

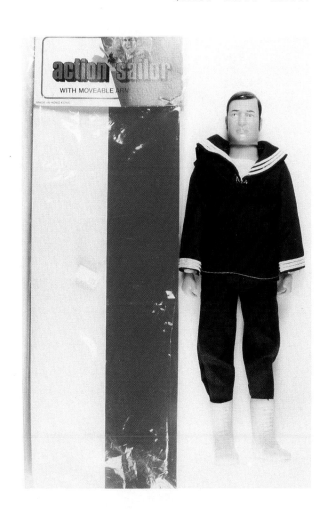

MADISON LTD.
Action Sailor. 11". Plastic body. Traditional navy uniform. Articulated at ankles, knees, hips, waist, shoulders, elbows, wrists, and neck. Black, molded hair, painted black eyes. Mark on back: Hong Kong. ca 1980.
$5.00 ~ 10.00 ~ 15.00.

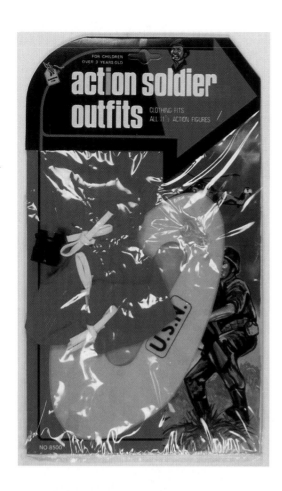

Madison Ltd. produced the following uniforms for its Action Figures titled "Action Soldier Outfits," No. 8500. There are no names for the outfits in the packages. The names are based on the items in the package at the discretion of the author.

MADISON LTD.

Sea Rescue. Package includes: traditional navy uniform of blue navy shirt with square collar, blue pants, black ankle shoes, orange vinyl vest marked: Air/ Vest/ U.S.A.F. 1980's.

$5.00 ~ 10.00 ~ 15.00.

MADISON LTD.

Navy Sentry. Package includes: traditional navy uniform of white sailor hat, blue navy shirt with square collar, blue pants, black ankle shoes, orange vinyl vest, pistol belt with pistol and holster. 1980's.

$5.00 ~ 10.00 ~ 15.00.

MADISON LTD.

Air Force Pilot. Package includes: gray zippered jumpsuit with two vertical red stripes, orange vinyl vest marked: Air/ Vest/ U.S.A.F., flare gun, white ankle shoes. 1980's.

$5.00 ~ 10.00 ~ 15.00.

MANUFACTURERS UNKNOWN
Nurse. 11". Thin hard plastic adult body. Articulated at hips, shoulders, and neck. Brown molded hair with molded ponytail. Painted black eyes with molded on eyelashes. Mark on back: Made in / Hong Kong. Dress tag: Made in / Hong Kong. 1950's.
$15.00 ~ 25.00 ~ 30.00.

MANUFACTURERS UNKNOWN
Nurse. 12½". Hard plastic teen body. Articulated at hips, shoulders, and neck. Glued on brown wig. Blue sleep eyes. Flat feet. Mark on back: O. ca. 1940.
$15.00 ~ 25.00 ~ 30.00.

MANUFACTURERES UNKNOWN
Sailor. 40". Doll marked 40-B inside arm. Mfg. Unk. 1960's. Authentic traditional navy uniform. Size 5. 1940's period. *(Author's collection.)*
$25.00 ~ 50.00 ~ 75.00.

MANUFACTURERS UNKNOWN
Sailor. 11". All composition body. Articulated at hips, shoulders, and neck. Blond glued on wig. Painted blue eyes. Marks: none. Dressed in an authentic traditional navy uniform made of original navy uniform fabric. ca. 1943.
$75.00 ~ 100.00.

══════ DOLLS NOT PICTURED ══════

MANUFACTURERS UNKNOWN
Sad Sack Soldier. 16". (Cartoon character by Sgt. George Parker.) U.S. Army uniform. Vinyl body. Articulated at neck. Molded on shoes. Painted features. (Sears catalog 1959.)
$100.00 – 150.00.

Dr. Ben Casey's Nurse. 11½". Plastic body. Dressed in a nurse's uniform with a cape. Molded hair. (Sears catalog 1963.)
$20.00 – 25.00 – 30.00.

Dr. Ben Casey. 12". Plastic body. Played on T.V. by Vince Edwards. (Good facial resemblance.) Molded hair. (Sears catalog 1963.)
$20.00 – 25.00 – 30.00.

Dr. Kildare. 12". Plastic body. Played on T.V. by Richard Chamberlain. (Good facial resemblance.) Molded hair. (Sears catalog 1963.)
$20.00 – 25.00 – 30.00.

Buddy Charlie. 12". Plastic body. In marine green camouflage fatigue uniform. (Ward's catalog 1966.)
$20.00 – 25.00 – 30.00.

Green Beret. 12". Green Beret dress in a class "A" uniform of the period. O.D. Ike jacket and pants, beret. Sold by Aldens for $4.99. (Aldens catalog 1966.)
$20.00 – 25.00 – 30.00.

Hombre. 12". Plastic body. Dressed in camouflage uniform with combat equipment. Ward's exclusive. Sold for $2.77. (Ward's catalog 1971.)
$20.00 – 25.00 – 30.00.

The Baron. 12". Plastic body. Dressed in a tank commander's uniform. Tan pants, leather type jacket with fur-trim collar, boots, goggles, pistol with holster and belt. Ward's exclusive. Sold for $2.46. (Ward's catalog 1972.)
$20.00 – 25.00 – 30.00.

Yankee Bravo code name for Secret Mission Man. 12". Plastic body. Dressed in O.D. beret, black sweater, camouflage pants, black boots, rifle, cartridge belt. Ward's exclusive. (Ward's catalog 1972.)
$20.00 – 25.00 – 30.00.

Green Beret. 12". Platic body. Dressed in a green Special Forces uniform. A Spiegel exclusive. (Spiegel catalog 1966.)
$20.00 – 25.00 – 30.00.

Big Red. 12". Plastic body. Wilderness Explorer. Articulated. A Spiegel exclusive. (Spiegel catalog 1973.)
$20.00 – 25.00 – 30.00.

MANUFACTURERS UNKNOWN
U.S.O. Hostess. 11". All composition body. Articulated at hips, shoulders, and neck. Blonde glued on wig. Painted blue eyes. Marks: none. Dressed in a pink satin ballroom gown, with a navy blue velvet cape and matching purse. ca. 1943.
$75.00 – 100.00.

MANUFACTURERS UNKNOWN
Airline Flight Attendant. 16". Thin plastic body and head. Articulated at hips, shoulders, and neck. Blonde molded on hair. Glued on reflective blue eyes. Mark on shoulders: Made in Hong Kong. 1950's.
$10.00 – 25.00.

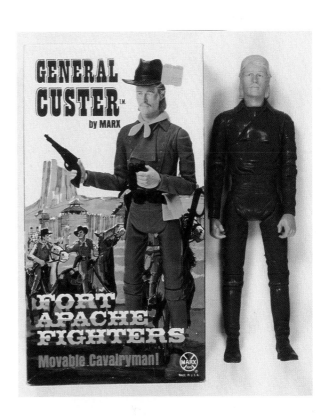

MANUFACTURERS UNKNOWN
Yankee Bravo. 11½". A Montgomery Ward's Exclusive. 1972.
$20.00 – 25.00 – 30.00.

MARX TOY
General Custer. 11½". Plastic body. Articulated at knees, hips, shoulders, elbows, wrists, and neck. Molded on cavalry blue uniform. Blond molded hair and moustache. Painted blue eyes. Mark in a circle on back: Louis Mark & Co. / © / MCMLXVII / Made In / U. S. A. 1967.
$30.00 – 75.00 – 100.00.

=== **DOLLS NOT PICTURED** ===

MARX TOY   *The Noble Knight Series*
The Black Knight. 11½". Plastic body. Articulated at knees, hips, waist, shoulders, elbows, wrists, and neck. Molded on black clothes. Black molded hair, moustache, goatee. Painted black eyes. 1967.
$50.00 – 100.00 – 125.00.

Tank Driver. 11½". Plastic body. Articulated at knees, hips, shoulders, elbows, wrists, and neck. Molded on O.D. uniform characterized by molded on tanker goggles on the molded on neck scarf. Molded on brown hair. Painted brown eyes. Mark on back: Marx / Toys. 1967.
$50.00 – 75.00 – 100.00.

Buck Hunter. 7½". Plastic body. Vinyl head. Articulated at knees, hips, shoulders, and neck. The right arm moves up and down by turning knob on his back. Brown molded hair. Painted brown eyes. Molded on khaki clothing and brown boots. Mark in a circle on back: Marx / Toys / Made in USA. ca. 1975.
$10.00 –25.00 – 30.00.

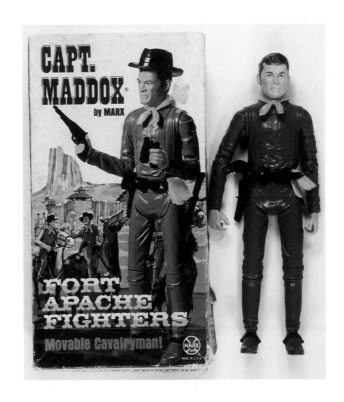

MARX TOY
Captain Maddox. 11½". Plastic body. Molded on blue cavalry uniform. Molded on brown hair. Painted brown eyes. Other characteristics same as General Custer. 1967.
$30.00 – 75.00 – 100.00.

Zeb Zachary Calvary Man. 11½". Plastic body. Description same as General Custer except for black molded hair, painted black eyes. 1967.

$30.00 ~ 75.00 ~ 100.00.

MARX TOY   *The Noble Knight Series*
Gordon the Gold Knight. 11½". Plastic body. Articulated at knees, hips, waist, shoulders, elbows, wrists, and neck. Molded on gold clothes. Brown molded hair, moustache, beard. Painted brown eyes. Mark same as Gen. Custer. 1967.
$50.00 ~ 100.00 ~ 125.00.

MARX TOY   *The Noble Knight Series*
Sir Stuart the Silver Knight. 11½". Plastic body. Description same as Gordon except for black molded hair, moustache, goatee. Painted black eyes and silver molded on clothes. 1967.
$50.00 ~ 100.00 ~ 125.00.

MARX TOY   *The Noble Knight Series*
Gordon the Gold Knight and Stuart the Silver Knight.

MARX TOY
Stony Stonewall Smith. 11½". Plastic body. Articulated at wrists, elbows, shoulders, and neck. Molded on O.D. army fatigues with the characteristic cargo pockets. Molded on paratrooper boots. Blond molded hair. Painted brown eyes. Mark in circle on back: Marx / Toys. 1967.
$40.00 ~ 75.00 ~ 100.00.

MARX TOY
Odin the Viking. 11½". Plastic body. Articulated same as Gordon. Brown molded hair and beard. Painted brown eyes. Molded on beige clothes. Mark same as Gordon. 1967.
$40.00 ~ 75.00 ~ 100.00.

MARX TOY
Eric the Viking. 11½". Plastic body. Articulation and mark same as Gordon. Molded on light green clothes. Blond molded hair and painted blue eyes. 1967.
$40.00 ~ 75.00 ~ 100.00.

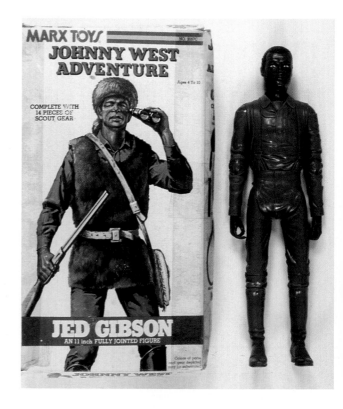

MARX TOY

Trooper Gibson (black). 9½". Plastic body. Vinyl head. Articulated at ankles, knees, hips, waist, shoulders, elbows, wrists, and neck. No hair (bald head). Painted black eyes. Marks: none. ca. 1982.

$80.00 ~ 175.00 ~ 200.00.

MARX TOY

Jed Gibson (black) Army Scout. 11½". Plastic body. Articulated at knees, hips, shoulders, elbows, wrists, and neck. Molded on blue cavalry uniform. Black molded hair. Painted black eyes. Mark in circle on back: Marx Toys / © / MCM-LXXIII / Made in / U.S.A. 1973.

$100.00 ~ 175.00 ~ 200.00.

MARX TOY

General Dwight D. Eisenhower. 11½". Plastic body. Articulated at ankles, knees, hips, waist, shoulders, elbows, wrists, and neck. Brown molded hair. Painted black eyes. Mark on the sole of the right foot in a circle: Made in Hong Kong / Marx / Toys. Same mark on the soles of both brown shoes and inside of the garrison cap. 1963.

$125.00 ~ 175.00 ~ 200.00.

MARX TOY
Buddy Charlie. 11½". Plastic body. Articulated at knees, hips, wrists, elbows, shoulders, and neck. Molded on O.D. class "A" uniform: "Ike" jacket with sergeant cheverons. Mark in circle on sole of right foot: Louis Marx Co. Inc. / © / MCMLXVII. Brown molded hair. Painted brown eyes. Molded on two buckle strap combat boots. 1967.
$50.00 – 75.00 – 100.00.

MARX TOY
Sgt. Kogo (black). 7½". Brown plastic body. Vinyl head. Articulated at knees, hips, shoulders, elbows, wrists, and neck. The right arm moves up and down by turning a knob on his back. Black molded hair. Painted black eyes. Molded on light blue t-shirt and Bermuda shorts. Molded on white knee stockings and brown ankle shoes. Mark in a circle on back: Marx / Toys / Made in USA. ©. 1975.
$10.00 – 25.00 – 30.00.

MATTEL INC.
9584 Barbie in Flight Time. 11½". Dressed in a bubble gum pink airline pilot's uniform. 1989. Back of package also shown.
$10.00 – 35.00 – 50.00.

MATTEL INC.

10688. Barbie Police Officer. 11½". Dressed in an authentic dark blue police officer's uniform. 1993.   **$10.00 ~ 35.00 ~ 50.00.**

MATTEL INC.

11581. Barbie and Ken Air Force Deluxe Set. 11½". Barbie dressed in an authentic U.S. Air Force "Thunderbird" red pilot's uniform. 1993. Ken, 12", dressed in an authentic U.S. Air Force "Thunderbird" dark blue pilot's uniform. 1993.

$10.00 ~ 35.00 ~ 50.00 ea.

MATTEL INC.
5626. Barbie and Ken Army Deluxe Set. 11½". Barbie dressed in an authentic desert camouflage battle dress uniform. 12". Ken dressed in an authentic desert camouflage battle dress uniform. 1992.

$10.00 ~ 35.00 ~ 50.00.

MATTEL INC.
7574. Ken Marine Corp. 12". Ken dressed in an authentic U.S. Marine Corp. dress blues uniform. 1991.

$10.00 ~ 35.00 ~ 50.00.

MATTEL INC.

7594. Barbie (black) Marine Corp. 11½".
Dressed in an authentic U.S. Marine Corp
dress blues uniform. 1991.

$10.00 ~ 35.00 ~ 50.00.

MATTEL INC.

7549. Barbie Marine Corp. 11½". Barbie
dressed in an authentic U.S. Marine Corp. dress
blues uniform. 1991.

$10.00 ~ 35.00 ~ 50.00.

9693. Barbie Navy. 11½". Barbie dressed in an authentic traditional U.S. Navy dress uniform. 1991.

$10.00 – 35.00 – 50.00.

3360. Barbie Air Force. 11½". Barbie dressed in an authentic U.S. Air Force pilot's uniform which includes a simulated leather jacket. 1990.

$10.00 – 35.00 – 50.00.

MATTEL INC.
3966. Barbie Army. 11½". Barbie dressed in an authentic U.S. Army Officer's evening dress uniform. 1989.

$10.00 ~ 35.00 ~ 50.00.

MATTEL INC.
4928. Barbie Canadian Mountie. 11½". Barbie dressed in an authentic Canadian Mountie uniform. 1987.

$15.00 ~ 50.00 ~ 75.00.

===== DOLLS NOT PICTURED =====

MATTEL INC.
The following uniforms were made for Barbie.
984. 1961. American Airlines Stewardess.

$50.00 ~ 75.00 ~ 100.00.

991. 1961. Registered Nurse.

$50.00 ~ 75.00 ~ 100.00.

1641. 1965. Miss Astronaut.

$50.00 ~ 75.00 ~ 100.00.

1678. 1966. Pan American Airways Stewardess.

$50.00 ~ 75.00 ~ 100.00.

7703. 1973. United Airlines Stewardess.

$50.00 ~ 75.00 ~ 100.00.

The following uniforms were made for Ken.
796. 1963. Sailor.

$50.00 ~ 75.00 ~ 100.00.

797. 1963. Army and Air Force.

$50.00 ~ 75.00 ~ 100.00.

0773. 1964. King Arthur.

$50.00 ~ 75.00 ~ 100.00.

0779. 1964. American Airlines Captain.

$50.00 ~ 75.00 ~ 100.00.

1415. 1965. Mr. Astronaut.

$50.00 ~ 75.00 ~ 100.00.

(Wards) 1967. Pilot Uniform.

$50.00 ~ 75.00 ~ 100.00.

7707. 1973. United Airlines Pilot outfit.

$50.00 ~ 75.00 ~ 100.00.

The following uniform was made for Francie.
7709. 1973. Candy Striper. (Mattel Fashion Booklets: 1961 – 1973.)

$50.00 ~ 75.00 ~ 100.00.

DOLLS NOT PICTURED

MATTEL INC.
Sgt. Storm Spaceman. 6". Flexible vinyl body with limbs enclosing a wire which permits easy flexing and posing at accordion like joints. Red space suit. 1966.

$50.00 ~ 100.00 ~ 125.00.

Jeff Long Spaceman (black). 6". Description same as Sgt. Storm except for face and blue space suit. 1966.

$100.00 ~ 250.00 ~ 300.00.

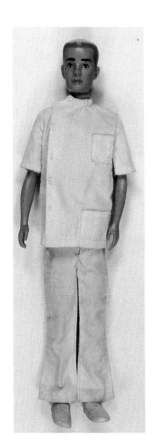

MATTEL INC.
0889. Candy Striper Volunteer. 1964. Manufactured for Barbie.

$50.00 ~ 75.00 ~ 100.00.

MATTEL INC.
#793. Dr. Ken. Tag: Ken T.M. / by Mattel. Mattel Inc. 1966.

$50.00 ~ 75.00 ~ 100.00.

MATTEL INC.
Major Matt Mason. (left) 6". Flexible vinyl body with limbs enclosing a wire which permits easy flexing and posing at accordion like joints. Molded white space suit. Mark on back: © 1966 Mattel Inc. / U.S. and Foreign / Patents Pending. (Note: See Colorform figures.) 1966.

$20.00 ~ 90.00 ~ 120.00.

Doug Davis Spaceman. (right) 6". Description same as Major Matt Mason except for face and orange or yellow spacesuit. 1966.

$50.00 ~ 150.00 ~ 200.00.

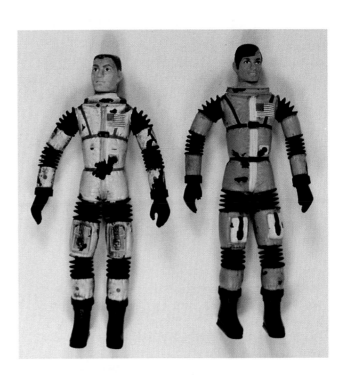

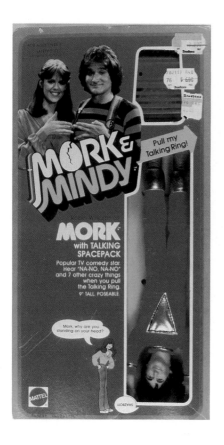

MATTEL INC.

1276. Mork Spaceman. 9". Plastic body. Vinyl head and arms. Articulated at knees, hips, shoulders, and neck. Brown molded hair. Painted blue eyes. Mark on head: © 1979 PPC Taiwan. Mark on body: © 1973 / Mattel Inc. / Taiwan. 1979.

$15.00 ~ 30.00 ~ 35.00.

MATTEL INC.   *Space 1999 Series*

9542. Commander Koenig. 9". Plastic body. Vinyl head and arms. Articulated at knees, hips, shoulders, and neck. Brown molded hair. Painted blue eyes. Mark on head: © 1975 ATV TM/ Licensing Ltd Taiwan. Mark on back: © 1973 / Mattel Inc. / Taiwan. 1975.

$15.00 ~ 35.00 ~ 50.00.

MATTEL INC.   *Space 1999 Series*

9543. Professor Bergman. 9". Description same as Commander Koenig except for gray receding molded hair. 1975.

$15.00 ~ 35.00 ~ 50.00.

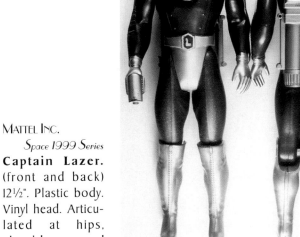

MATTEL INC. *Space 1999 Series*

Captain Lazer. (front and back) 12½". Plastic body. Vinyl head. Articulated at hips, shoulders, and neck. Molded on blue space suit. Molded gray space boots. Mark on lower back: © 1967 Mattel Inc. / Hawthorne Cal. / Made in Mexico. Molded on gray battery pack. Eyes and gun light up. 1967.

$100.00 ~ 150.00 ~ 200.00.

MATTEL INC. *Space 1999 Series*

9544. Doctor Russell. 8½". Plastic adult female body. Vinyl head and arms. Articulated at knees, hips, shoulders, and neck. Brown molded hair. Painted blue eyes. Marks same as Commander Koenig. 1975.

$15.00 ~ 35.00 ~ 50.00.

MATTEL INC. *Battlestar Galactica*

2536. Colonial Warrior. 12½". Plastic body. Vinyl head. Articulated at knees, hips, shoulders, and neck. Molded on cream-colored space suit with gray legs. Molded on black boots. (Same mold as for Capt. Lazer.) Blond molded hair. Painted blue eyes. Mark on lower body: © Mattel Inc. / 1967. 1978 U.S.A. Molded on black battery pack on back. 1978.

$20.00 ~ 75.00 ~ 100.00.

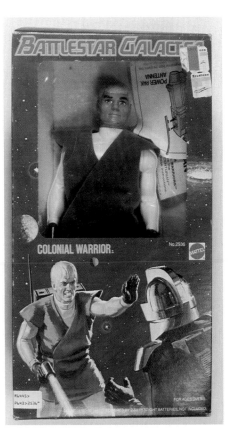

MATTEL   *Battlestar Galactica*

2537. Cylon Centurian. 12½". All black plastic body. Characteristics same as Colonial Warrior except molded on chrome metallic helmet. 1978.

$20.00 ~ 75.00 ~ 100.00.

MATTEL INC.

Julia Nurse. 11½". Brown plastic body. Played on T.V. by Diahann Carroll. Vinyl head and legs. Articulated at hips, waist, shoulders, and neck. Has bendable knees. Reddish black rooted hair. Painted brown eyes. High heel feet. Mark on back: ©1965 / Mattel Inc. / U.S. Patented / U.S. Pat. Pend. / Made in Japan. 1965.

$50.00 ~ 120.00 ~ 150.00.

MEGO

1100. Action Jackson. 8". Plastic body. Vinyl head. Articulated at ankles, knees, hips, waist, shoulders, and neck. Black molded hair. Painted black eyes. Mark on shoulder blades: © Mego Corp. / Reg. U.S. Pat. Off. / Pat. Pend. / Hong Kong / MCMLXXI. 1971.

$10.00 ~ 25.00 ~ 30.00.

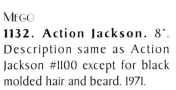

MEGO

1132. Action Jackson. 8". Description same as Action Jackson #1100 except for black molded hair and beard. 1971.

$10.00 ~ 25.00 ~ 30.00.

MEGO

1133. Action Jackson. (black) 8". Description same as Action Jackson #1100 except for brown plastic body, black molded hair. 1971.

$25.00 ~ 50.00 ~ 75.00.

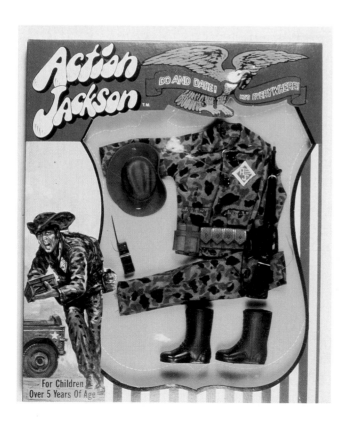

The following uniforms were produced by the Mego Company for Action Jackson.

MEGO

1101. Aussie Marine. Package includes: green plastic campaign hat, green camouflaged fatigue jacket and pants, green cartridge belt, green British style canteen and case, handie talkie, M-16 rifle, black ankle shoes. 1971.

$10.00 ~ 25.00 ~ 30.00.

MEGO

1102. Air Force. Package includes: gray flight helmet with visor, gray flight suit, white belt, black ankle shoes, orange "Mae West" air vest, pistol, and shoulder holster. 1971.

$10.00 – 25.00 – 30.00.

MEGO

1103. Navy. Package includes: traditional white sailor's hat, blue navy shirt with square collar and pants, white cartridge belt, black ankle shoes, binoculars, M-16 rifle. 1971.

$10.00 – 25.00 – 30.00.

MEGO

1104. Frogman. Package includes: orange hooded vinyl SCUBA suit, black face mask, black swim fins, gray SCUBA air tanks with mouth piece, red buoy, blinker light, spear gun. 1971.

$10.00 – 25.00 – 30.00.

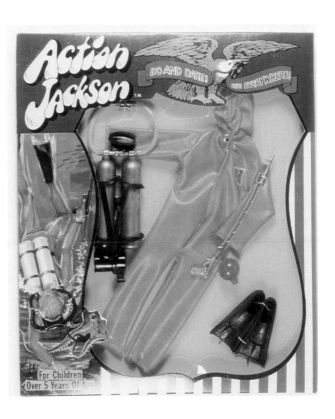

MEGO

1105. Ski-Patrol. Package includes: white hooded cloth jumpsuit, white ankle shoes, white cartridge belt, white British style canteen and case, white radio, white skies and ski poles, black M-16 rifle. 1971.

$10.00 ~ 25.00 ~ 30.00.

MEGO

1106. Army. Package includes: green army helmet, O.D. Ike style jacket and pants, black ankle shoes, green cartridge belt, green British style canteen and case, black M-16 rifle. 1971.

$10.00 ~ 25.00 ~ 30.00.

MEGO

1107. Rescue Squad. Package includes: silver metallic hood, silver metallic jumpsuit, gray ankle boots, grappling hook with rope, axe, pliers. 1971.

$10.00 ~ 25.00 ~ 30.00.

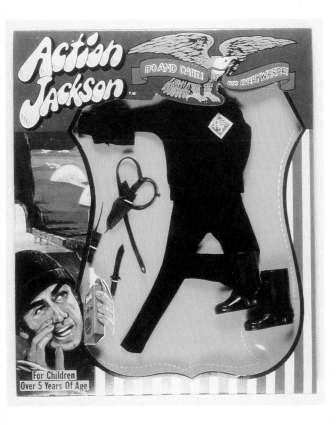

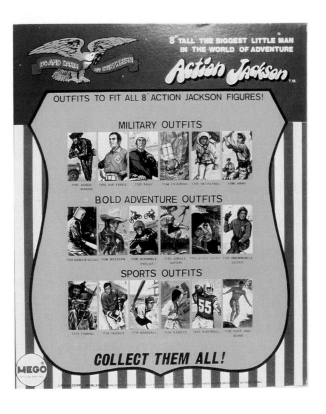

Action Jackson uniform package back.

1111 Signal Spy. Package includes: black cloth knit sailor's hat, black sweater and pants, black ankle shoes, handie talkie, knife, pistol, and shoulder holster. 1971.

$10.00 ~ 25.00 ~ 30.00.

8" Action Jackson. Note the articulation of the three figures. The two on the left are held by metal rivets. The one on the right is held by molded plastic knobs. Mego Corp.

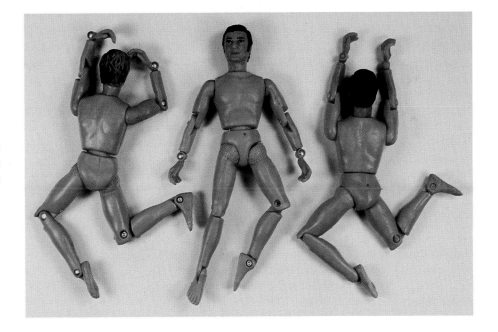

MEGO

1133 Action Jackson. 8". Plastic body. Vinyl head. Articulated at ankles, knees, hips, waist, shoulders, and neck. Blond molded hair. Painted black eyes. Mark on shoulder blades: © Mego Corp. / Reg. U.S. Pat. Off. / Pat. Pend. / Hong Kong / MCM-LXXI. 1971.

$10.00 ~ 25.00 ~ 30.00.

Action Jackson. 8". Description same as Action Jackson #1133 except for blond molded hair and beard. 1971.

$10.00 ~ 25.00 ~ 30.00.

Action Jackson. 8". Description same as Action Jackson #1133 except for brown molded hair. 1971.

$10.00 ~ 25.00 ~ 30.00.

Action Jackson. 8". Description same as Action Jackson #1133 except for brown molded hair and beard. 1971.

$10.00 ~ 25.00 ~ 30.00.

Action Jackson (black). 8". Description same as Action Jackson #1133 except for brown plastic body, black molded hair and beard. 1971.

$25.00 ~ 50.00 ~ 75.00.

51203/2. The Keeper. 8". Plastic body. Vinyl head. Articulated at ankles, knees, hips, waist, shoulders, and neck. Blue ridged head and face. Mark on head: © Paramount / Pict. Corp. 1975.

$80.00 ~ 190.00 ~ 200.00.

California Highway Patrol Series.
Ponch CHIPS. 8". Description same as Action Jackson #1133 except face. 1978.

$20.00 ~ 40.00 ~ 50.00.

Jon CHIPS. 8". Description same as Action Jackson #1133 except face and mark on head: MGM / NC 1977. 1978.

$20.00 ~ 40.00 ~ 50.00.

Sarge CHIPS. 8". Description same as Action Jackson #1133 except face. 1978.

$20.00 ~ 40.00 ~ 50.00.

The following two listings are from the Star Trek the Movie Series.
Decker. 12½". Description same as Buck Rogers except face, brown molded hair, painted brown eyes, mark on head: © PPC. 1979.

$50.00 ~ 125.00 ~ 150.00.

Klingon Commander. 12½". Plastic body. Vinyl head. Articulated at ankles, knees, hips, waist, shoulders, elbows, wrists, and neck. Black molded hair. Klingon head with black molded hair, painted brown eyes, mark on head: © PPC. 1979.

$50.00 ~ 100.00 ~ 125.00.

Richie (black). 12". Plastic body. Fully articulated. Dark brown sprayed flocked hair, painted black eyes. Mark on back: Mego / MCMLXX / Made in Hong Kong. 1970.

$10.00 ~ 25.00 ~ 30.00.

Richie. 12". Description same as above except for light brown sprayed flocked hair. 1970.

$10.00 ~ 25.00 ~ 30.00.

The following seven listings are the uniforms made by Mego Corp. for its Fighting Yank and all 12" action figures.
3303. Army Military Police. Package includes: white helmet, khaki jacket and pants, M.P. arm band, white pistol belt, pistol and holster, clipboard, billy club, black low quarter shoes. 1970.

$10.00 ~ 25.00 ~ 30.00.

3304. Air Force Flight Uniform. Package includes: white flight helmet with visor, gray flight jumpsuit, white pistol belt, pistol and holster, clipboard, orange air vest marked Air / Vest, black ankle shoes. 1970.

$10.00 ~ 25.00 ~ 30.00.

3310. Air Force Dress Uniform. Package includes: blue garrison cap, blue U.S. Air Force dress jacket and pants, black low quarter shoes. 1970.

$10.00 ~ 25.00 ~ 30.00.

3311. Marine Dress Uniform. Package includes: white garrison cap, blue U.S. Marine dress jacket with red trim, blue U.S. Marine dress pants with red stripe, white pistol belt, white U.S. M-1 rifle. 1970.

$10.00 ~ 25.00 ~ 30.00.

3312. Army Green Beret Uniform. Package includes: O.D. green helmet, green fatigue jacket and pants, O.D. cartridge belt, hand grenades, black ankle shoes, brown U.S. M-1 rifle. 1970.

$10.00 ~ 25.00 ~ 30.00.

3313. Navy Dress Uniform. Package includes: white sailor hat, blue sailor shirt with square collar with white trim, blue pants, white cartridge belt, black ankle shoes, brown U.S. M-1 rifle. 1970.

$10.00 ~ 25.00 ~ 30.00.

3330. West Point Cadet. Package includes: white garrison cap with black bill, blue West Point style jacket with gold trim, white pants with blue stripe, black low quarter shoes. 1970.

$10.00 ~ 25.00 ~ 30.00.

MEGO *Planet of the Apes Series (movie)*
1965 Astronaut. 8". Plastic body. Vinyl head. Description same as Action Jackson except for face, brown molded hair, painted blue eyes. Mark on head: © Mego Corp / 1972.
$40.00 – 90.00 – 120.00.

MEGO *Planet of the Apes Series (movie)*
1964. Ape Soldier. 8". Plastic body. Vinyl head. Description same as Action Jackson except for ape features of head and mark on head © APJAC Prod. Inc. & / 20th Century - Fox Film Corp. 1974.
$40.00 – 75.00 – 100.00.

MEGO *Planet of the Apes Series (movie)*
1962. Dr. Zaius. Mego Corp. 1974.
$50.00 – 100.00 – 150.00.

MEGO   *Star Trek Series*
51200/1. Captain Kirk. 8". Description same as Action Jackson except for face and mark on head: © Paramount / Pict. Corp. 1973.

$20.00 ~ 50.00 ~ 60.00.

MEGO   *Star Trek Series*
51200/3 Dr. McCoy. 8". Description same as Captain Kirk except for face. 1973.

$20.00 ~ 60.00 ~ 70.00.

MEGO   *Star Trek Series*
51200/5 Mr. Scott (Scottie). 8". Description same as Captain Kirk except for face. 1973.

$20.00 ~ 60.00 ~ 75.00.

MEGO   *Star Trek Series*
51200/2 Mr. Spock. 8". Description same as Captain Kirk except for face. 1973.

$20.00 ~ 50.00 ~ 60.00.

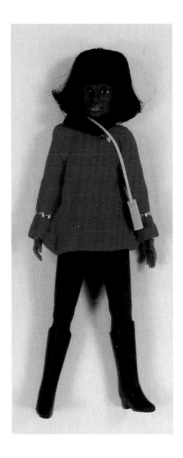

MEGO   *Star Trek Aliens Series*
51203/3. The Gorn. 8". Description same as Captain Kirk except for brown alligator head and face. 1975.
                    $80.00 ~ 190.00 ~ 200.00.

MEGO   *Star Trek Series*
51200/4. Lt. Uhura. 8". Mark on head: © 1974 / Paramount / Pict. Corp. Mark on shoulder blades: © Mego Corp / MCM-LXXII / Pat. Pending / Made in / Hong Kong. 1974.
                    $20.00 ~ 40.00 ~ 60.00.

MEGO   *Star Trek Series*
51200/7. Klingon. 8". Description same as Captain Kirk except face. 1973.
                    $30.00 ~ 60.00 ~ 75.00.

MEGO   *Star Trek Aliens Series*
Package back of Star Trek Aliens Series.

MEGO   *Star Trek Aliens Series*
51203/4. Cheron. 8". Description same as Captain Kirk except right side of the body is black and the left side is white. 1975.
$75.00 ~ 120.00 ~ 130.00.

MEGO   *Star Trek Aliens Series*
51203/1. Neptunian. 8". Description same as Captain Kirk except for green head and face. 1975.
$80.00 ~ 190.00 ~ 200.00.

MEGO   *Star Trek Aliens Series*
51204/1. The Romulan. 8". Description same as Captain Kirk except for face. 1976.
$275.00 ~ 400.00 ~ 425.00.

MEGO   *Star Trek Aliens Series*
51204/3. Andorian. 8". Description same as Captain Kirk except for white head with horns and white face. 1976.
$190.00 ~ 310.00 ~ 325.00.

MEGO   *Star Trek Aliens Series*
51204/4. Mugato. 8". Description same as Captain Kirk except for a single orange horn and an orange ape-like face. 1976.

$150.00 ~ 275.00 ~ 300.00.

MEGO   *Star Trek Aliens Series*
51204/2. Talos. 8". Description same as Captain Kirk except for head with greatly enlarged frontal area and face. 1976.
$150.00 ~ 225.00 ~ 250.00.

MEGO   *Camelot Series*

51000/1. King Arthur. 8". Description same as Action Jackson except for face and mark on head: ©
Mego Corp 1973. 1974.

$50.00 – 100.00 – 125.00.

MEGO   *Camelot Series*

51000/3. Sir Galahad. 8".
Description same as Action Jackson except for face and mark on
head: © 1974. Mego Corp. 1974.

$50.00 – 100.00 – 125.00.

MEGO   *Camelot Series*

51000/4. Sir Lancelot. 8". Description same as Action Jackson except face and mark on head: ©
1974. Mego Corp. 1974.

$50.00 ~ 100.00 ~ 150.00.

MEGO   *Camelot Series*

51000/5. Black Knight. 8".
Description same as Action Jackson except face and mark on
head: © Mego Corp. 1974.

$50.00 ~ 125.00 ~ 200.00.

MEGO   *Camelot Series*

51000/6. Ivanhoe. 8". Description same as Action Jackson except face and mark on head: © 1974. Mego Corp. 1974.

$50.00 ~ 100.00 ~ 150.00.

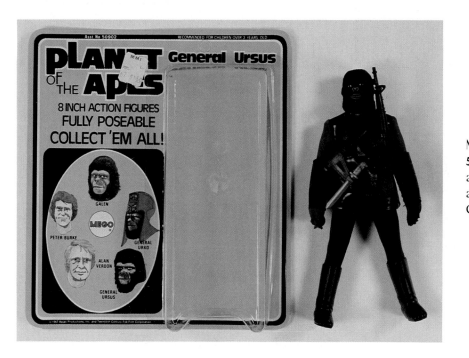

MEGO   *Planet of the Apes Series (T.V.)*

50900/7 General Ursus. 8". Description same as Action Jackson except ape features of head and mark on head: © APJAC Prod. Inc. & 20th Century - Fox Film Corp. 1974.

$50.00 ~ 100.00 ~ 150.00

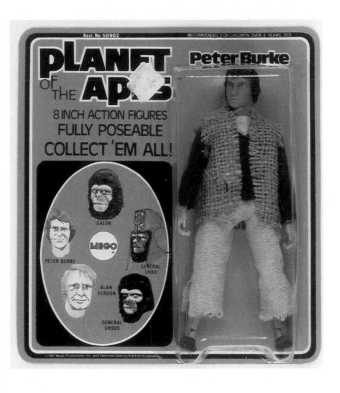

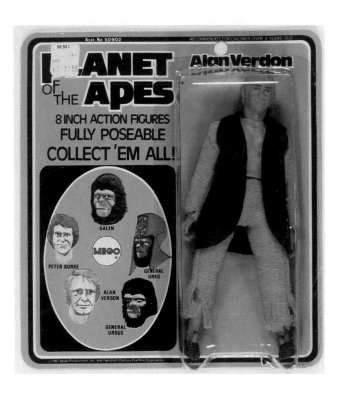

MEGO   *Planet of the Apes Series (T.V.)*
50900/9. Peter Burke Astronaut. 8". Mego Corp. 1974.
$50.00 ~ 125.00 ~ 150.00.

MEGO   *Planet of the Apes Series (T.V.)*
50900/0. Alan Verdon Astronaut. Mego Corp. 1974.
$50.00 ~ 125.00 ~ 150.00.

MEGO   *Planet of the Apes Series (T.V.)*
50900/8. General Urko. 8". Description same as
Action Jackson except for ape features of head and
mark on head: © APJAC Prod. Inc. & / 20th Century - Fox Film Corp. 1974.
$40.00 ~ 100.00 ~ 150.00.

MEGO   *Flash Gordon Series*
74400/1. Flash Gordon. 9½". Plastic body. Vinyl head. Articulation similar to Action Jackson. Mark on head: King Features / Syn Inc. 1976. Mark on back: 1976 Mego Corp. / Made in Hong Kong. 1977.
$25.00 ~ 75.00 ~ 100.00.

MEGO   *Flash Gordon Series*
74400/2. Ming the Merciless. 9½". Description same as Flash Gordon except for face. 1977.
$25.00 ~ 75.00 ~ 100.00.

MEGO   *Flash Gordon Series*
74400/3. Dr. Zarkov. 9½". Description same as Flash Gordon except for face. 1977.
$25.00 ~ 75.00 ~ 100.00.

MEGO   *Flash Gordon Series*

74400/3. Dale Arden.
9". Plastic body. Vinyl
head and poseable legs.
Articulated at waist,
shoulders, elbows, wrists,
and neck. Mark on head:
King Features / Syn Inc.
1976. Mark on back: 1977
Mego Corp / Made in
Hong Kong. 1977.

**$25.00 – 60.00 –
100.00.**

MEGO   *Flash Gordon Series*
Package back.

MEGO   *Superman Series*

87003/3. General Zod.
12½". Plastic body. Vinyl
head. Articulated at ankles,
knees, hips, waist, shoulders,
elbows, wrists, and neck.
Black molded hair and beard.
Painted blue eyes. Mark on
head: © D.C. Comics Inc. /
1977. Mark on back: © Mego
Corp. 1977 / Made in Hong
Kong. 1977.

$25.00 – 65.00 – 80.00.

MEGO *Buck Rogers Series*

Buck Rogers. 12½". Plastic body. Vinyl head. Articulated at ankles, knees, hips, waist, shoulders, elbows, wrists, and neck. Black molded hair. Painted blue eyes. Mark on head: © 1978 Robert / C. Dille. Mark on body: © 1978 Mego Corp. / Made in Hong Kong. 1978.

$25.00 ~ 50.00 ~ 60.00.

MEGO *Buck Rogers Series*

Dr. Huer. 12½". Description same as Buck Rogers except face, brown molded hair, painted blue eyes. 1978.

$25.00 ~ 50.00 ~ 60.00.

MEGO *Buck Rogers Series*
Killer Kane. 12½". Description same as Buck Rogers except face, brown molded hair, painted blue eyes. 1978.
$25.00 ~ 50.00 ~ 60.00.

MEGO *Buck Rogers Series*
Draconian Guard. 12½". Description same as Buck Rogers except face, brown molded hair and beard, painted brown eyes. 1978.
$25.00 ~ 60.00 ~ 75.00.

MEGO   *Buck Rogers Series*

Draco. 12½". Description same as Buck Rogers except face, gray molded hair, black molded moustache and goatee. Painted brown eyes. 1978.

$25.00 ~ 50.00 ~ 60.00.

MEGO   *Buck Rogers Series*

Tiger Man. 12½". Description same as Buck Rogers except face, bald head with black streaks, black moustache, painted brown eyes. 1978.

$25.00 ~ 60.00 ~ 75.00.

MEGO   *Buck Rogers Series*
Package back.

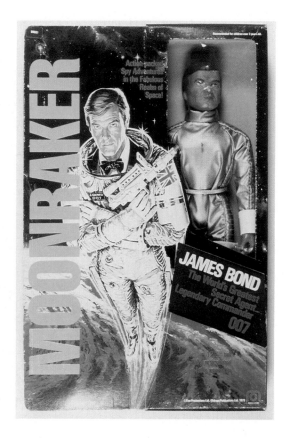

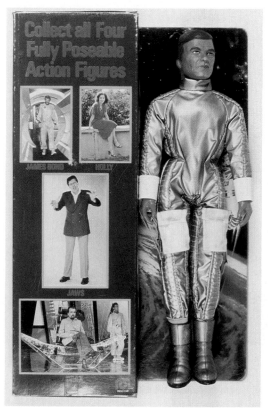

MEGO   *Moonraker Series*
James Bond. 12½". Description same as Buck Rogers except face, brown molded hair, painted blue eyes, mark on head: © 1979 EON / Productions Ltd. 1979.

$25.00 ~ 60.00 ~ 75.00.

MEGO   *Star Trek the Movie Series*
Captain Kirk. 12½". Description same as Buck Rogers except face, brown molded hair, painted blue eyes, mark on head: © PPC. 1979.

$20.00 ~ 50.00 ~60.00.

MEGO   *Star Trek the Movie Series*

Mr. Spock. 12½". Description same as Buck Rogers except face, pointed ears, black molded hair, painted brown eyes, mark on head: © PPC. 1979.

$20.00 – 50.00 – 60.00.

MEGO   *Star Trek the Movie Series*

Ilia. 12½". Plastic adult female body. Vinyl bald head. Bendable arms and legs. Articulated at hips, waist, shoulders, wrists, and neck. Painted brown eyes. Mark on head: © PPC. Mark on lower back: © Mego Corp. 1975 / Made in Hong Kong. 1979.

$20.00 – 50.00 – 60.00.

MEGO   *Star Trek the Movie Series*

Package back.

MEGO   *Star Trek the Movie Series*

Acturian. 12½". Description same as Buck Rogers except Acturian head with no hair, painted brown eyes, brown colored body, mark on head: © PPC. 1979.

$50.00 – 75.00 – 100.00.

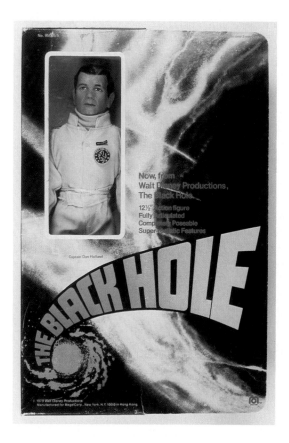

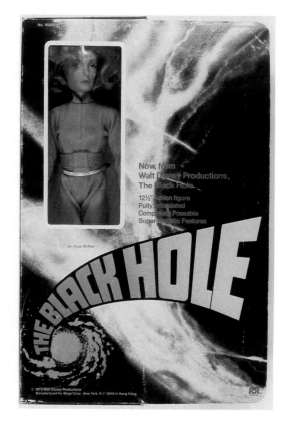

MEGO   *The Black Hole Series*
95005/5 Captain Dan Holland. 12½". Description same as
Buck Rogers except face, black molded hair, painted brown
eyes, mark on head: © Walt Disney / Productions 1979.

$20.00 – 50.00 – 60.00.

MEGO   *The Black Hole Series*
95005/1. Dr. Kate McRae. 12½". Plastic adult female body
with the same characteristics as Ilia except face and auburn
rooted hair, mark on head: © Walt Disney / Productions
1979.

$25.00 – 75.00 – 100.00.

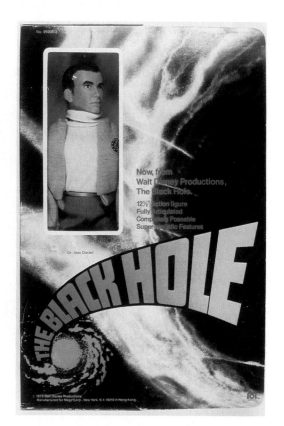

MEGO   *The Black Hole Series*
95005/2. Dr. Alex Durant. 12½". Description same as Captain Holland except face. 1979.

$20.00 – 60.00 – 70.00.

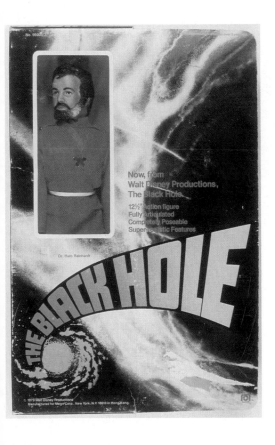

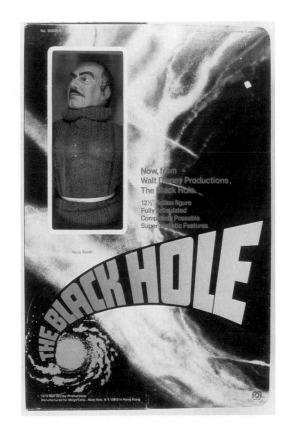

MEGO   *The Black Hole Series*
95005/3. Dr. Hans Reinhardt. 12½". Description same as Captain Holland except face, brown molded hair and beard. 1979.

$20.00 ~ 60.00 ~ 70.00.

MEGO   *The Black Hole Series*
95005/4. Harry Booth. 12½". Description same as Captain Holland except face, graying black molded hair, and black moustache. 1979.

$20.00 ~ 60.00 ~ 70.00.

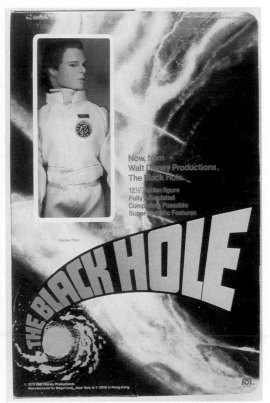

MEGO   *The Black Hole Series*
Package back.

MEGO   *The Black Hole Series*
95005/6. Charles Pizer. 12½". Description same as Captain Holland except face and molded brown hair. 1979.

$20.00 ~ 60.00 ~ 70.00.

MEGO

Wonder Woman as Lt. Diane Prince U.S. Navy. 12½". Plastic adult female body with the same description as Ilia except face, black rooted hair, mark on head: © D.C. Comics / Inc. 1976, and painted on Wonder Woman costume on body. (Note: The first Wonder Woman of this series had a fabric costume.) Package includes complete woman's naval uniform of the period. 1976.

$80.00 ~ 125.00 ~ 150.00.

MEGO

73500/1. Wonder Woman 12½". Was first sold with a fabric costume, second with a painted on costume with painted on blue tights with stars, third with a painted on costume and blue fabric tights (shown above). 1976.

$80.00 ~ 125.00 ~ 150.00.

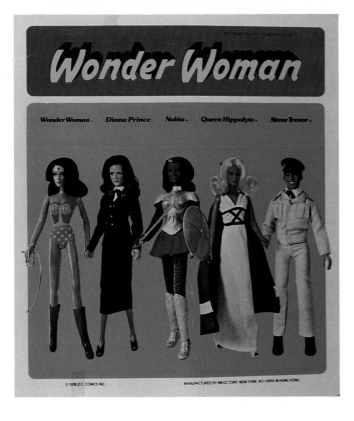

MEGO
Package back.

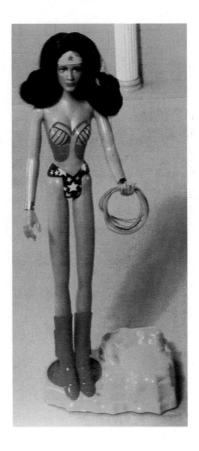

MEGO
Wonder Woman. 12¼". 73500/1 in a permanent and completely painted on costume. Mego Corp. 1977.

   $80.00 ~ 125.00 ~ 150.00.

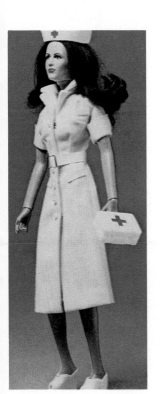

MEGO
Wonder Woman. 12½". 73500/1 in nurse uniform #73525. Mego Corp. 1977.

   $20.00 ~ 30.00 ~ 40.00.

MEGO
Nubia in warrior uniform. Wonder Woman's super foe. 12½". Brown plastic adult female body with the same description as Ilia except face, black rooted hair, mark on head: © D.C. Comics / Inc. 1976.

   $25.00 ~ 75.00 ~ 100.00.

Mego
Steve Trevor Major U.S. Army. 12½". Description same as Captain Holland except face, mark on head: © 1976 D C / Comics Inc. 1976.

$25.00 ~ 75.00 ~ 100.00.

Mego
Queen Hippolyte. 12½". #73500/5. Wonder Woman. Mego Corp. 1976.

$25.00 ~ 75.00 ~ 100.00.

Mego
Fighting Yank. 12". Plastic body. Vinyl head and arms with wire inside. Articulated at ankles, knees, hips, waist, shoulders, and neck. Brown molded hair. Painted black eyes. Mark on back: © Mego R / MCMLXX / Made in Hong Kong. Dog Tag: Fighting / Yank. 1970.

$10.00 ~ 25.00 ~ 30.00.

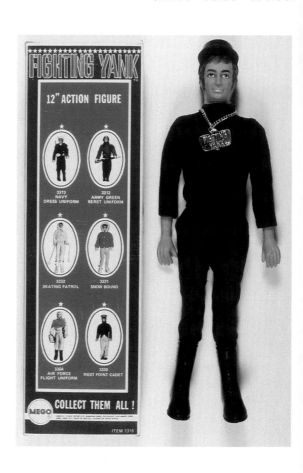

Mego
Fighting Yank.
Package back.

The Mego Corp. made the following uniforms for its Fighting Yank and all 12" action figures. The uniform accessory packages are titled Fighting Yank.

MEGO
3301. Navy Frogman. Package includes: green camouflage swim suit, face mask, snorkel, wrist watch, diving knife, SCUBA air tanks with mouth piece, swim fins, yellow inflatable raft marked: U.S.N. 1970.

$10.00 – 25.00 – 30.00.

MEGO
3331. Snow Bound. Package includes: red fur-trimmed hooded parka, yellow ski styled pants, white ankle snow boots. 1970.

$10.00 – 25.00 – 30.00.

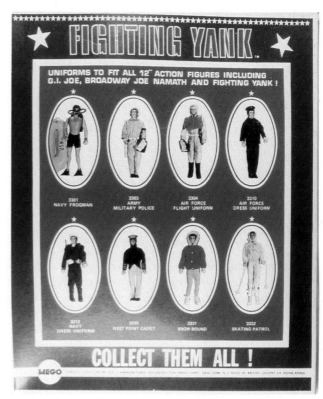

MEGO

3332. Skating (sic) Patrol. Should be Skiing Patrol. Package includes: white hooded parka, white ski style pants, white ankle snow boots, white skis, white ski poles. 1970.

$10.00 ~ 25.00 ~ 30.00.

MEGO

5644. Diver. 8½". Plastic body. Articulated at shoulders and neck. Brown molded hair. Painted black eyes. Mark on back: Blue Box / Toy / - in a circle - Hong Kong. (Diver's suit is made of sewn vinyl plastic. It is similar to G.I. Joe's™ diver suit.) 1977.

$10.00 ~ 30.00 ~ 35.00.

═══ DOLLS NOT PICTURED ═══

MOLLYE

Chris. The American Airlines Stewardess. 14". Hard plastic body. Articulated at hips, shoulders, and neck. Blonde rooted hair. Blue sleep eyes. Mark: none. Clothes tag: Hollywood Cinema Fashions. Mark on box: Mollye creations. "Authentically dressed." Designed by: International Doll Co. Philadelphia, PA.
$25.00 ~ 100.00 ~ 150.00.

Chris. 18". Description same as 14" Chris.
$25.00 ~ 110.00 ~ 160.00.

Chris. 24". Description same as 14" Chris.
$25.00 ~ 120.00 ~ 170.00.

Chris. 18". Description same as 14" Chris.
$25.00 ~ 130.00 ~ 180.00.

MOR-TOYS

8005. Johnny Strong. 12". Plastic body. Articulated at hips, shoulders, and neck. Black molded hair. Painted brown eyes. Mark on back: Made in Hong Kong. ca. 1977.
$10.00 ~ 20.00 ~ 25.00.

NORMA ORIGINALS INC.

Girl Scout. 11½". Plastic body. Articulated at neck, hips, and shoulders. Blonde glued-on hair. Painted right-looking blue eyes. Wearing 1940 intermediate Girl Scout uniform. ca. 1950.
$25.00 ~ 50.00.

PENGO INTERNALTIONAL TOYS

Action Buddy. 11½". Plastic body. Articulated at knees, hips, and shoulders. Brown molded hair. Painted black eyes. Mark: none. ca. 1977.
$10.00 ~ 20.00 ~ 25.00.

RED BOX

5644. Marine. 8½". Plastic body. Articulated at shoulders and neck. Brown molded hair. Painted black eyes. Mark on back: Blue Box / Toy / - in a circle - Hong Kong. Uniform: traditional naval officer's khaki uniform of the period with garrison cap. Wears orange air vest. 1977.
$10.00 ~ 30.00 ~ 35.00.

5644. Commando. 8½" Description same as Marine. Uniform: U.S. Army O.D. fatigue type of the period. 1977.
$10.00 ~ 30.00 ~ 35.00.

5644. Sailor. 8½". Description same as Marine. Uniform: British traditional navy blue uniform with black banded white hat. 1977.
$10.00 ~ 30.00 ~ 35.00.

RELIABLE TOY COMPANY

R.A.F. Flyer of WWII. 18". Composition head and arms. Cloth body. Light brown molded hair. Painted brown eyes. Mark: Reliable / Made in / Canada. ca. 1942. *(Courtesy Patricia R. Smith, Doll Values #1, pg. III.)*
$50.00 ~ 200.00 ~ 250.00.

Military Man Army. 14". Characteristics same as R.A.F. Flyer. ca. 1942.
$50.00 ~ 200.00 ~ 250.00.

Mountie. 17". Characteristics same as R.A.F. Flyer. ca. 1942.
$50.00 ~ 200.00 ~ 250.00.

REMCO

1415. Dr. John's Medical Tunic and Slacks. Remco made this doctor's uniform for Dr. John Littlechap. Package includes: white cloth tunic and slacks, white socks, white shoes, stethoscope, tongue depressor, fountain pen, wristwatch, and doctor's bag. 1963.
$10.00 ~ 50.00 ~ 60.00.

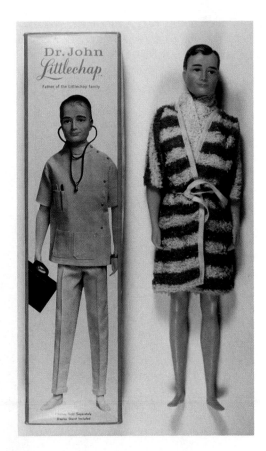

REMCO

Dr. John Littlechap. 15". Plastic body. Vinyl head and arms. Articulated at hips, shoulders, and neck. Black molded hair with a touch of gray. Painted black eyes. Mark on back in a circle: Dr. / John / Littlechap / Remco Industries / © 1963.
$20.00 ~ 50.00 ~ 60.00.

═══ DOLLS NOT PICTURED ═══

ROBERTA
Dr. Ben Casey's Nurse. 17". Plastic body. Vinyl head and arms. Dark brown rooted hair. Blue sleep eyes. Mark: none. Dress Tag: Dr. Ben Casey / Roberta. 1963. *(Courtesy Patricia R. Smith. Modern Collector's Dolls #2, pg 294.)*

$10.00 ~ 20.00 ~ 40.00.

Dr. Kildare's Nurse. 13". Plastic body. Vinyl head and arms. Blonde rooted hair. Blue sleep eyes. Mark on head: AE 153 / 14. 1964. *(Courtesy Patricia R. Smith. Modern Collector's Dolls #2, pg. 294)*

$10.00 ~ 20.00 ~ 40.00

M.S. SHILLMSN, INC.
G.I. Fighting Ace. 12". Plastic body. Vinyl head. Articulated at ankles, knees, hips, waist, shoulders, and neck. Black molded hair. Painted on brown eyes. Mark on back: Made in / Hong Kong. 1974.

$10.00 ~ 25.00 ~ 30.00.

The following accessory uniforms were made by the Shillman company for G.I. Fighting Ace.
Military Police outfit. Package includes: white helmet, brown Ike styled jacket and pants, white pistol belt with pistol and holster, M.P. arm band, billy club. 1974.

$10.00 ~ 25.00 ~ 30.00.

Marine Dress set. Package includes: white garrison cap, blue marine style dress jacket with red piping, blue dress pants with red stripe along side, black shoes, white U.S. M-I rifle. 1974.

$10.00 ~ 25.00 ~ 30.00.

Camouflage outfit. Package includes: green camouflage helmet, green camouflage fatigue jacket and pants, black ankle shoes. 1974.

$10.00 ~ 25.00 ~ 30.00.

Air Force outfit. Package includes: blue garrison cap, light blue shirt, dark blue tie, blue dress jacket and pants, black shoes, clipboard. 1974.

$10.00 ~ 25.00 ~ 30.00.

Astronaut outfit. Package includes: silver metallic hood with window, silver metallic jacket, silver metallic pants, and gloves. (Similar to fire fighter's outfit in G.I. Joe's™ Crash Crew.) 1974.

$10.00 ~ 25.00 ~ 30.00.

Combat Flyer Outfit. Package includes: flight helmet, gray flight jumpsuit, pistol belt with pistol and holster, orange vinyl "Mae West" air vest. 1974.

$10.00 ~ 25.00 ~ 30.00.

M.S. SHILLMAN, INC.
G.I. Fighting Ace. 12". Plastic body. Vinyl head. Articulated at ankles, knees, hips, waist, shoulders, and neck. Black molded hair. Painted brown eyes. Mark on back: Made in / Hong Kong. 1974.

$10.00 ~ 25.00 ~ 30.00.

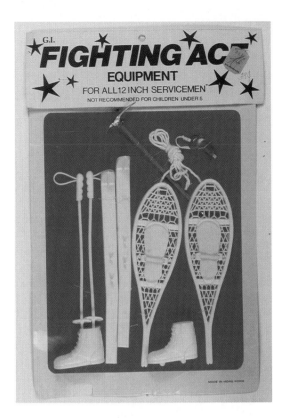

M.S. SHILLMAN, INC.
Equipment accessories for the G.I. Fighting Ace.

=============== DOLLS NOT PICTURED ===============

SHINDANA
Wanda Career Girl Nurse. 9". Brown plastic body. Vinyl head, arms, and legs. Articulated at hips, waist, shoulders, and neck. Black rooted hair. Painted brown eyes. Mark on back: © 1972 / Shindana Toys / Hong Kong. 1972.

$10.00 – 25.00 – 30.00.

SHINDANA
Wanda Stewardess. 9". Brown plastic body. Vinyl head, arms, and legs. Articulated at hips, waist, shoulders, and neck. Black rooted hair. Painted brown eyes. Mark on back: © 1972 / Shindana Toys / Hong Kong. 1972.

$10.00 – 25.00 – 30.00.

DOLLS NOT PICTURED

TERRI LEE
Terri Lee Girl Scout. 8". (The Terri Lee Co. purchased Ginger from the Cosmopolitan Co. for this series.) Hard plastic body. Articulated at hips, shoulders, and neck. Brown glued on wig. Blue sleep eyes. Mark on vinyl head: Ginger. 1956.
$20.00 – 50.00 – 75.00.

Terri Lee Brownie. 8". Description same as Terri Lee Girl Scout except in a Brownie uniform. 1956.
$20.00 – 50.00 – 75.00.

Terri Lee Blue Bird. 8". Description same as Terri Lee Girl Scout except in a Blue Bird uniform. 1956.
$20.00 – 50.00 – 75.00.

Terri Lee Camp Fire Girl. 8". Description same as Terri Lee Girl Scout except in a Camp Fire Girl uniform. 1956.
$20.00 – 50.00 – 75.00.

Terri Lee Girl Scout. 16". Hard plastic body. Articulated at hips, shoulders, and neck. Brown glued on wig. Blue sleep eyes. Mark on back: Terri Lee. 1955.
$20.00 – 50.00 – 75.00.

Terri Lee Brownie. 16". Description same as 16" Terri Lee Girl Scout except in Brownie uniform. 1955.
$20.00 – 50.00 – 75.00.

Terri Lee Blue Bird. 16". Description same as 16" Terri Lee Girl Scout except in Blue Bird uniform. 1955.
$20.00 – 50.00 – 75.00.

Terri Lee Camp Fire Girl. 16". Description same as 16" Terri Lee Girl Scout except in Camp Fire Girl uniform. 1955.
$20.00 – 50.00 – 75.00.

TOPPER TOYS   *The Tigers Series*
Machine Gun Mike. 6½". Plastic body. Articulated at shoulders and neck. All Tigers have a mechanical right arm which is released by pressing a button located between the shoulder blades. Blond molded hair. Painted brown eyes. Mark on head: DLR © / 1966. Mark on body: Deluxe Reading Corp. / Elizabeth, N. J. / © 1966. Specialty: Raising machine gun.
$10.00 – 25.00 – 30.00.

TOPPER TOYS   *The Tigers Series*
Bugle Ben. 6½". Description same as Machine Gun Mike except dark brown molded hair slicked back. Specialty is raising a bugle to his lips. 1966.
$10.00 – 25.00 – 30.00.

TOPPER TOYS   *The Tigers Series*
Pretty Boy. 6½". Description same as Machine Gun Mike except face, black molded crew cut hair with a widow's peak. Specialty is raising arm to salute. 1966.
$10.00 – 25.00 – 30.00.

The following uniform accessory packages were produced by
Topper Toys for The Tigers. The packages were called Official
Accessory Kit.

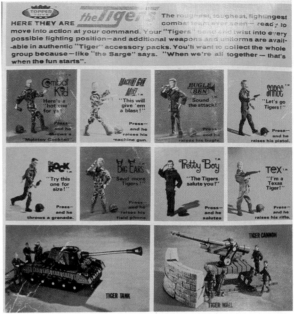

TOPPER TOYS
PG 0596. Official Accessory Kit. Package includes: olive drab class "A" uniform with
brass buttons and brass collar insignias, O.D. helmet, white shirt, black tie, walkie talkie,
bugle, 45 caliber pistol.

$15.00 – 25.00 – 35.00.

TOPPER TOYS
PG 0598. Official Accessory Kit. Package
includes: olive drab combat fatigues, O.D. helmet, entrenching shovel, hand grenade, 30 caliber M-l carbine.

$15.00 – 25.00 – 35.00.

================ DOLLS NOT PICTURED ================

TOPPER TOYS   *The Tigers Series*

Tex. 6½". Plastic body. Articulated at shoulders and neck. All Tigers have a mechanical right arm which is released by pressing a button located between the shoulder blades. Blond molded hair with a point coming above the left eye. Painted brown eyes. Specialty is raising a rifle. Mark on head: DLR © / 1966. Mark on body: Deluxe Reading Corp. / Elizabeth, N.J. / © 1966.
$10.00 – 25.00 – 30.00.

The Rock. 6½". Description same as Tex except black molded hair in a flat top crew cut. Specialty is raising arm to throw a grenade. 1966.
$10.00 – 25.00 – 30.00.

Combat Kid. 6½". Description same as Tex except blond molded hair. Specialty is raising arm to throw Molotov cocktail. 1966.
$10.00 – 25.00 – 30.00.

Sarge. 6½". Description same as Tex except face, brown molded short crew cut hair. Specialty is raising a pistol. 1966.
$10.00 – 25.00 – 30.00.

Big Ear. 6½". Description same as Tex except face, exaggerated ears, and sparse brown molded hair. Specialty is raising a walkie-talkie. 1966.
$10.00 – 25.00 – 30.00.

TOPPER TOYS
Connie. 6". #0512-0001. Majorette. Topper Toys. 1971.
$10.00 – 25.00 – 35.00.

TOPPER TOYS
Dawn. 6". #0511 - 0001. Majorette. Topper Toys. 1971.
$10.00 – 25.00 – 35.00.

TOPPER TOYS
Kip. 6". #0513 - 0001. Majorette. Topper Toys. 1971.
$10.00 – 25.00 – 35.00.

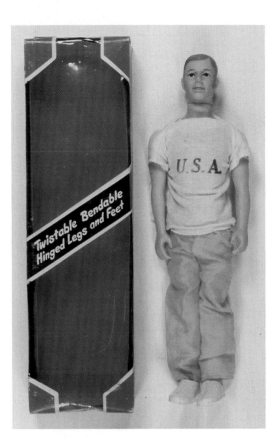

TOPPER TOYS
Side View of packages for the Dawn Majorette Series. Topper Toys. 1971.

TOTSY TOY COMPANY
C2002. Bill Champ. 12". Plastic body. Vinyl head. Articulated at ankles, knees, hips, waist, shoulders, and neck. Blond molded hair. Painted blue eyes. Mark on shoulder blades: Made in Hong Kong. 1970. Original outfit: white t-shirt, yellow sweat pants, white low quarter shoes. Box illustrated with a running soldier with rifle and fixed bayonet.

$10.00 ~ 25.00 ~ 30.00.

TOTSY TOY COMPANY
C2002. Bill Champ. 12". Description same as Bill Champ above except brown molded hair. 1970.

$10.00 ~ 25.00 ~ 30.00.

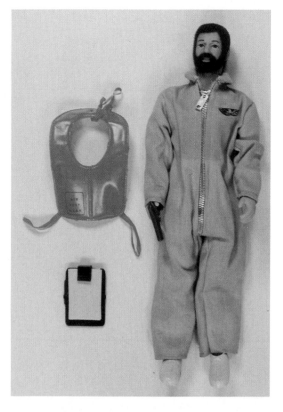

Totsy Toy Company
C2002. Bill Champ. 12". Description same as Bill Champ (previous page) except flocked brown hair and beard. 1970.

$10.00 ~ 25.00 ~ 30.00.

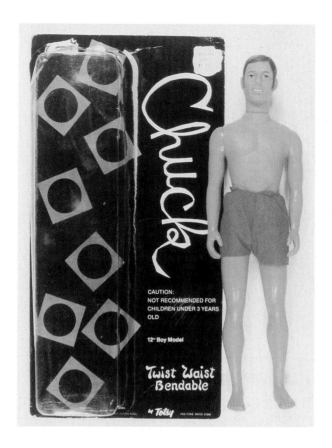

Totsy Toy Company
Chuck Boy model. 12". Description same as Bill Champ except brown molded hair. 1970.

$10.00 ~ 25.00 ~ 30.00.

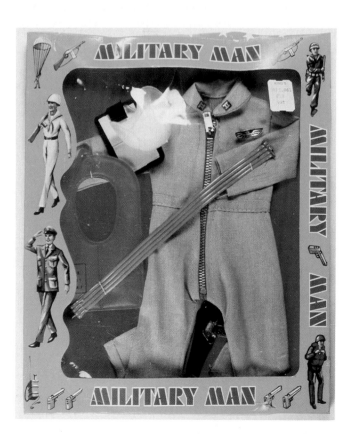

Totsy Toy Company
C2001. U.S. Air Force pilot uniform. Package includes: white flight helmet, gray flight jumpsuit, O.D. pistol belt with pistol and holster, black clipboard, orange "Mae West" air vest marked Air / Vest / U.S.A.F. 1970.

$10.00 ~ 25.00 ~ 30.00.

DOLLS NOT PICTURED

TOTSY TOY COMPANY
Chuck Boy model. 12". Plastic body. Vinyl head, arms, and legs. Articulated at hips, waist, shoulders, and neck. Blond molded hair. Painted blue eyes. Mark on back: Hong Kong. 1970.
$10.00 ~ 25.00 ~ 30.00.

The following military uniforms were made for Bill Champ, Chuck, and other 11½" – 12" action figures. The earlier accessory packages were titled Bill Champ with lot No. C2001 and the later packages were titled Military Man with no numbers.

C2001 U.S. Navy Shore Patrol. Package includes: white helmet, blue traditional navy shirt with square collar and blue pants, pistol belt with pistol and holster, billy club. 1970.
$10.00 ~ 25.00 ~ 30.00.

C2001 U.S. Air Force dress uniform. Package includes: blue garrison cap, white shirt, black tie, blue dress jacket, and blue pants. 1970.
$10.00 ~ 25.00 ~ 30.00.

C2001. On Guard U.S. Navy sailor uniform. Package includes: white helmet, white traditional navy shirt with square collar and white pants, U.S. M-1 carbine. 1970.
$10.00 ~ 25.00 ~ 30.00.

TOTSY TOY COMPANY
Accessory package: Equipment. Bill Champ. Totsy Toy Co. 1970.
$10.00 ~ 25.00 ~ 30.00.

The Totsy Toy Company made the following accessory package for Military Man.

TOTSY TOY COMPANY
Military Man field accessories. Package includes: tent, tent poles and stakes, blanket, canteen, mess kit, entrenching shovel, U.S. M-1 carbine. 1970.
$10.00 ~ 25.00 ~ 30.00.

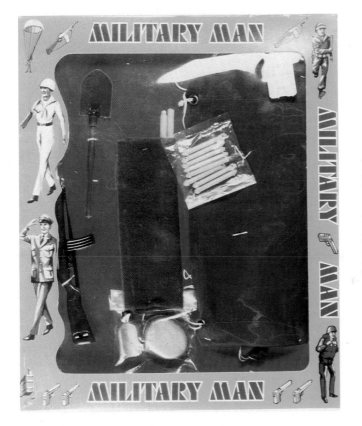

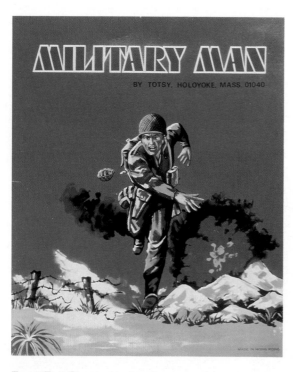

TOTSY TOY COMPANY
Military Man field accessories. Package back.

VICTORIA TOY WORKS, WELLING-
TON, SHROPSHIRE, ENGLAND
Norah Wellings
Sailor. 8½". Cloth body. Painted on features on a molded and
stiffened fabric. Right-looking
blue eyes. Velvet-like material
for the uniform. Cotton fabric
for the collar and hat. Hat band:
Empress of Canada. 1960's.
$15.00 ~ 50.00 ~ 100.00.

<hr>

DOLLS NOT PICTURED

VICTORIA TOY WORKS — NORA WELLINGS
Canadian Mountie. 8½". Cloth body. Painted on features on a
molded and stiffened fabric. Right-looking blue eyes. Canadian
Mountie uniform. ca. 1960's.
$15.00 ~ 50.00 ~ 100.00.

VOGUE DOLL INC.
W.A.A.C. 13". Composition body. Articulated at hips, shoulders,
and head. Blonde glued on wig. Painted right-looking blue eyes.
Mark: none. ca. 1942.
$25.00 ~ 100.00 ~ 150.00.

W.A.V.E. 13". Composition body. Articulated at hips, shoulders,
and head. Brown glued on wig. Painted right-looking blue eyes.
Mark: none. ca. 1942.
$25.00 ~ 100.00 ~ 150.00.

Toddles Soldier. 8". In army uniform. Composition body. Articulated at hips, shoulders, and neck. Blond glued on wig. Painted
right-looking blue eyes. Mark on head: Vogue. Mark on back:
Doll Co. 1943.
$25.00 ~ 50.00 ~ 75.00.

Toddles Sailor. 8". Description same as Toddles Soldier, except
a navy uniform. 1943.
$25.00 ~ 50.00 ~ 75.00.

Toddles Aviator. 8". Description same as Toddles Soldier,
except an aviator uniform of the period. 1943.
$25.00 ~ 50.00 ~ 75.00.

Toddles Navy Captain. 8". Description same as Toddles Soldier, except in a naval officer's uniform. 1943.
$25.00 ~ 50.00 ~ 75.00.

Toddles Nurse. 8". Toddles in a white nurse's uniform. 1943.
$25.00 ~ 50.00 ~ 75.00.

31. Ginny Nurse. 8". Ginny in a white nurse's uniform which
includes; white nurse's cap, white socks, and white shoes. Hard
plastic body. Articulated at hips, shoulders, and neck. Blonde
glued on wig. Blue sleep eyes. Mark on head: Vogue. Mark on
back: Vogue Doll, Inc. / Pat. Pend. / Made in U.S.A. 1954.
$20.00 ~ 35.00 ~ 50.00.

31. Ginny Nurse. 8". Ginny in a white nurse's uniform #31.
Description same as 1954 Ginny Nurse except mark on back: Ginny
/ Vogue Dolls, Inc. / Pat. No. 2687594 / Made in U.S.A. 1955.
$20.00 ~ 35.00 ~ 50.00.

VOGUE DOLL INC.
7032. Ginny Brownie. 8". Ginny in a Brownie uniform which includes a brown Brownie dress and beany, brown socks and shoes. Description same as 1954 Ginny Nurse. 1955.

$20.00 ~ 35.00 ~ 50.00.

WORLD DOLLS COMPANY
Wac, #8000, Wave #8001. 18". Created by doll artist and sculptor Sandra Blake. 1988. The dolls are the creative property of World Dolls Company, New York, with all rights reserved. Photograph used with permission.

$150.00 ~ 250.00 ~ 300.00.

═══════════ DOLLS NOT PICTURED ═══════════

FOREIGN COMPANIES
Mrs. Andrew Nurse. 18". Plastic body. Articulated at hips, shoulders, neck. Light brown molded hair. Inset blue eyes. Mark: / Made in Hong Kong. Original uniform includes white nurse uniform, white nurse cap, white shoes. Nurse to the quintuplet babies. ca. 1938. *(Courtesy Patricia R. Smith. Modern Collector's Dolls #4, pg 94.)*

$10.00 ~ 25.00 ~ 50.00.

(RT) HONG KONG   *Heroes of the American Revolution*

George Washington. 8". Plastic body. Articulated at hips, waist, shoulders, and neck. White molded hair. Painted blue eyes. Mark on back: Made in / Hong Kong. (Note: Inside some of the coats in this series is a sewn in tag: © MEGO ® / Hong Kong.) 1975.

$20.00 ~ 75.00 ~ 100.00.

 HONG KONG   *Heroes of the American Revolution*

Nathan Hale. 8". Plastic body. Description same as Washington except face, black molded hair, and painted brown eyes. 1975.

$20.00 ~ 50.00 ~ 65.00.

(R T) HONG KONG   *Heroes of the American Revolution*

Thomas Jefferson. 8". Plastic body. Description same as Washington except face, blond molded hair, and painted blue eyes. 1975.

$20.00 ~ 50.00 ~ 65.00.

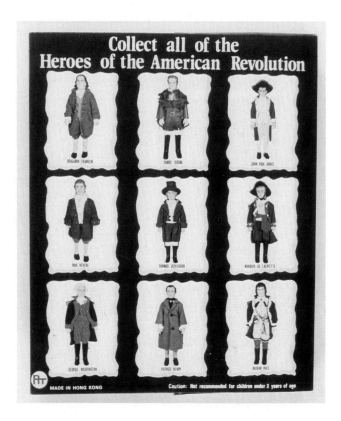

(R T) HONG KONG   *Heroes of the American Revolution*

Thomas Jefferson. Package back.

 HONG KONG   *Heroes of the American Revolution*

Benjamin Franklin. 8". Plastic body. Description same as Washington except face, black molded hair, and painted blue eyes. 1975.

$20.00 – 50.00 – 65.00.

 HONG KONG   *Heroes of the American Revolution*

Daniel Boone. 8". Plastic body. Description same as Washington except face, light brown molded hair, and painted blue eyes. 1975.

$20.00 – 50.00 – 65.00.

 HONG KONG   *Heroes of the American Revolution*

Marquis de LaFayette. 8". Plastic body. Description same as Washington except face, blond molded hair, and painted brown eyes. 1975.

$20.00 – 50.00 – 65.00.

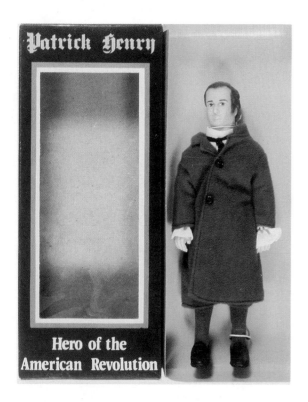

Ⓡ⊤ HONG KONG   *Heroes of the American Revolution*

Patrick Henry. 8". Plastic body. Description same as Washington except face, dark brown molded hair, and painted brown eyes. 1975.

$20.00 ~ 50.00 ~ 65.00.

Ⓡ⊤ HONG KONG   *Heroes of the American Revolution*

Paul Revere. 8". Plastic body. Description same as Washington except face, light brown molded hair, and painted blue eyes. 1975.

$20.00 ~ 50.00 ~ 65.00.

Ⓡ⊤ HONG KONG   *Heroes of the American Revolution*

John Paul Jones. 8". Plastic body. Description same as Washington except face, black molded hair, and painted blue eyes. 1975.

$20.00 ~ 50.00 ~ 65.00.

Note: All bubble packages marked: UA/75526.

UNIVERSAL COMPANY, HONG KONG   *The 1776 People*

Continental Soldier 1776. 8". Plastic body. Articulated at knees, double articulation at hips (can sit on a horse), waist, shoulders, elbows, middle of upper arm, and neck. Brown molded hair. Painted brown eyes. Mark on back: U. S. A. & U. K. / Pat. Pending / Tong Ind. Co. / Hong Kong. 1976.
$20.00 ~ 50.00 ~ 65.00.

UNIVERSAL COMPANY, HONG KONG   *The 1776 People*

British Soldier 1776. 8". Plastic body. Description same as Continental Soldier except blond molded hair. 1976.
$20.00 ~ 50.00 ~ 65.00.

UNIVERSAL COMPANY, HONG KONG   *The 1776 People*

Hessian Soldier 1776. 8". Plastic body. Description same as Continental Soldier except dark brown molded hair and painted brown eyes. 1976.

$20.00 – 50.00 – 65.00.

COMPANY UNKNOWN, HONG KONG   *Spirit of '76*

Drummer Man. 8". Plastic body. Articulated at hips, waist, shoulders, neck. Long brown molded hair. Painted brown eyes. Mark on back: Made in / Hong Kong. 1976.

$20.00 – 50.00 – 65.00.

COMPANY UNKNOWN, HONG KONG *Spirit of '76*

Fifer Man. 8". Plastic body. Description same as Drummer Man except face, long black hair and beard, and painted blue eyes. 1976.

$20.00 ~ 50.00 ~ 65.00.

COMPANY UNKNOWN, HONG KONG *Spirit of '76*

Drummer Boy. 8". Plastic body. Description same as Drummer man except face and short brown molded hair. 1976.

$20.00 ~ 50.00 ~ 65.00.

Born in Fitchburg, MA, in 1929, Joseph G.L. Bourgeois is a retired high school teacher. He earned a Bachelor of Science degree in 1960, and a Master of Education degree in science in 1968.

In the early 1940's Joe was an enthusiastic participant in the Boy Scouts. He enlisted in the U.S. Army in 1947, and served a peaceful tour of duty in Korea with the 7th Infantry Division. In 1950 he re-enlisted in the U.S. Army and served with the 3rd Infantry division in Korea, where he earned the Combat Infantryman Badge.

After the army Joe attended the University of Massachusetts in Amherst where he met his future wife Ann C. Sheehy. They were married in 1960, and are the parents of two boys, Joseph and Paul.

Joe in his Boy Scout uniform, 1943.

Joe at his desk at Randolph High School.
(Courtesy Stephany Snyder 1990.)

Joe taught young people biology, ecology, earth science, and meteorology in Massachusetts for 32 years, first in Taunton and then in Randolph.

Among his many many interests are camping, fishing, gardening, bird watching, competitive pigeon racing, and collecting dolls in military uniforms. In 1964 Joe purchased his first G.I. Joe for his son Joe, and the rest is history. He has been collecting ever since and has contributed a short article on G.I. Joe in Patricia R. Smith's 3rd volume of *Modern Collector Dolls*. Another short article on Mego dolls was published in Patricia R. Smith's 4th volume of *Modern Collector Dolls*.

BOOKS ON COLLECTIBLES

This is only a partial listing of the books on antiques that are available from Collector Books. All books are well illustrated and contain current values. Most of the following books are available from your local bookseller, antique dealer, or public library. If you are unable to locate certain titles in your area, you may order by mail from COLLECTOR BOOKS, P.O. Box 3009, Paducah, KY 42002-3009. Customers with Visa or MasterCard may phone in orders from 7:00–4:00 CST, Monday–Friday, Toll Free 1-800-626-5420. Add $2.00 for postage for the first book ordered and $0.30 for each additional book. Include item number, title, and price when ordering. Allow 14 to 21 days for delivery.

DOLLS, FIGURES & TEDDY BEARS

2382	**Advertising Dolls**, Identification & Values, Robison & Sellers	$9.95
2079	**Barbie** Doll Fashions, Volume I, Eames	$24.95
3957	**Barbie** Exclusives, Rana	$18.95
3310	**Black Dolls**, 1820–1991, Perkins	$17.95
3873	**Black Dolls**, Book II, Perkins	$17.95
3810	**Chatty Cathy** Dolls, Lewis	$15.95
2021	Collector's **Male Action Figures**, Manos	$14.95
1529	Collector's Encyclopedia of **Barbie** Dolls, DeWein	$19.95
3727	Collector's Guide to **Ideal Dolls**, Izen	$18.95
3728	Collector's Guide to Miniature **Teddy Bears**, Powell	$17.95
4506	**Dolls in Uniform**, Bourgeois	$18.95
3967	Collector's Guide to **Trolls**, Peterson	$19.95
1067	**Madame Alexander** Dolls, Smith	$19.95
3971	**Madame Alexander** Dolls Price Guide #20, Smith	$9.95
2185	**Modern Collector's** Dolls I, Smith	$17.95
2186	**Modern Collector's** Dolls II, Smith	$17.95
2187	**Modern Collector's** Dolls III, Smith	$17.95
2188	**Modern Collector's** Dolls IV, Smith	$17.95
2189	**Modern Collector's** Dolls V, Smith	$17.95
3733	**Modern Collector's** Dolls, Sixth Series, Smith	$24.95
3991	**Modern Collector's** Dolls, Seventh Series, Smith	$24.95
3472	**Modern Collector's** Dolls Update, Smith	$9.95
3972	Patricia Smith's **Doll Values**, Antique to Modern, 11th Edition	$12.95
3826	Story of **Barbie**, Westenhouser	$19.95
1513	**Teddy Bears & Steiff** Animals, Mandel	$9.95
1817	**Teddy Bears & Steiff** Animals, 2nd Series, Mandel	$19.95
2084	**Teddy Bears, Annalee's & Steiff** Animals, 3rd Series, Mandel	$19.95
1808	Wonder of **Barbie**, Manos	$9.95
1430	World of **Barbie** Dolls, Manos	$9.95

TOYS, MARBLES & CHRISTMAS COLLECTIBLES

3427	**Advertising Character** Collectibles, Dotz	$17.95
2333	Antique & Collector's **Marbles**, 3rd Ed., Grist	$9.95
3827	Antique & Collector's **Toys**, 1870–1950, Longest	$24.95
3956	**Baby Boomer Games**, Identification & Value Guide, Polizzi	$24.95
1514	**Character Toys** & Collectibles, Longest	$19.95
1750	**Character Toys** & Collector's, 2nd Series, Longest	$19.95
3717	**Christmas** Collectibles, 2nd Edition, Whitmyer	$24.95
1752	**Christmas** Ornaments, Lights & Decorations, Johnson	$19.95
3874	Collectible **Coca-Cola** Toy **Trucks**, deCourtivron	$24.95
2338	Collector's Encyclopedia of **Disneyana**, Longest, Stern	$24.95
2151	Collector's Guide to **Tootsietoys**, Richter	$16.95
3436	Grist's Big Book of **Marbles**	$19.95
3970	Grist's Machine-Made & Contemporary **Marbles**, 2nd Ed.	$9.95
3732	**Matchbox**® Toys, 1948 to 1993, Johnson	$18.95
3823	**Mego** Toys, An Illustrated Value Guide, Chrouch	15.95
1540	**Modern Toys** 1930–1980, Baker	$19.95
3888	**Motorcycle** Toys, Antique & Contemporary, Gentry/Downs	$18.95
3891	Schroeder's Collectible **Toys**, Antique to Modern Price Guide	$17.95
1886	Stern's Guide to **Disney** Collectibles	$14.95
2139	Stern's Guide to **Disney** Collectibles, 2nd Series	$14.95
3975	Stern's Guide to **Disney** Collectibles, 3rd Series	$18.95
2028	**Toys**, Antique & Collectible, Longest	$14.95
3975	**Zany Characters** of the Ad World, Lamphier	$16.95

JEWELRY, HATPINS, WATCHES & PURSES

1712	Antique & Collector's **Thimbles** & Accessories, Mathis	$19.95
1748	Antique **Purses**, Revised Second Ed., Holiner	$19.95
1278	**Art Nouveau & Art Deco Jewelry**, Baker	$9.95
3875	Collecting Antique **Stickpins**, Kerins	$16.95
3722	Collector's Ency. of **Compacts, Carryalls & Face Powder Boxes**, Mueller	$24.95
3992	Complete Price Guide to **Watches**, #15, Shugart	$21.95
1716	Fifty Years of Collector's **Fashion Jewelry**, 1925-1975, Baker	$19.95
1424	**Hatpins** & Hatpin Holders, Baker	$9.95
1181	100 Years of Collectible **Jewelry**, Baker	$9.95
2348	20th Century Fashionable Plastic **Jewelry**, Baker	$19.95
3830	Vintage **Vanity Bags & Purses**, Gerson	$24.95

FURNITURE

1457	American **Oak** Furniture, McNerney	$9.95
3716	American **Oak** Furniture, Book II, McNerney	$12.95
1118	Antique **Oak** Furniture, Hill	$7.95
2132	Collector's Encyclopedia of **American** Furniture, Vol. I, Swedberg	$24.95
2271	Collector's Encyclopedia of **American** Furniture, Vol. II, Swedberg	$24.95
3720	Collector's Encyclopedia of **American** Furniture, Vol. III, Swedberg	$24.95
1437	Collector's Guide to **Country** Furniture, Raycraft	$9.95
3878	Collector's Guide to **Oak** Furniture, George	$12.95
1755	Furniture of the **Depression Era**, Swedberg	$19.95
3906	**Heywood-Wakefield** Modern Furniture, Rouland	$18.95
1965	**Pine** Furniture, Our American Heritage, McNerney	$14.95
1885	**Victorian** Furniture, Our American Heritage, McNerney	$9.95
3829	**Victorian** Furniture, Our American Heritage, Book II, McNerney	$9.95
3869	**Victorian** Furniture books, 2 volume set, McNerney	$19.90

INDIANS, GUNS, KNIVES, TOOLS, PRIMITIVES

1868	Antique **Tools**, Our American Heritage, McNerney	$9.95
2015	Archaic **Indian** Points & Knives, Edler	$14.95
1426	**Arrowheads** & Projectile Points, Hothem	$7.95
1668	**Flint Blades** & Projectile Points of the North American Indian, Tully	$24.95
2279	**Indian** Artifacts of the Midwest, Hothem	$14.95
3885	**Indian** Artifacts of the Midwest, Book II, Hothem	$16.95
1964	**Indian** Axes & Related Stone Artifacts, Hothem	$14.95
2023	**Keen Kutter** Collectibles, Heuring	$14.95
3887	Modern **Guns**, Identification & Values, 10th Ed., Quertermous	$12.95
2164	**Primitives**, Our American Heritage, McNerney	$9.95
1759	**Primitives**, Our American Heritage, Series II, McNerney	$14.95
3325	Standard **Knife** Collector's Guide, 2nd Ed., Ritchie & Stewart	$12.95

PAPER COLLECTIBLES & BOOKS

1441	Collector's Guide to **Post Cards**, Wood	$9.95
2081	Guide to Collecting **Cookbooks**, Allen	$14.95
3969	Huxford's **Old Book** Value Guide, 7th Ed.	$19.95
3821	Huxford's **Paperback** Value Guide	$19.95
2080	Price Guide to **Cookbooks** & Recipe Leaflets, Dickinson	$9.95
2346	**Sheet Music** Reference & Price Guide, Pafik & Guiheen	$18.95

OTHER COLLECTIBLES

2280	Advertising **Playing Cards**, Grist	$16.95
2269	Antique **Brass & Copper** Collectibles, Gaston	$16.95
1880	Antique **Iron**, McNerney	$9.95
3872	Antique **Tins**, Dodge	$24.95
1714	**Black** Collectibles, Gibbs	$19.95
1128	**Bottle** Pricing Guide, 3rd Ed., Cleveland	$7.95
3959	**Cereal Box** Bonanza, The 1950's, Bruce	$19.95
3718	Collector's **Aluminum**, Grist	$16.95
3445	Collectible **Cats**, An Identification & Value Guide, Fyke	$18.95
1634	Collector's Ency. of Figural & Novelty **Salt & Pepper Shakers**, Davern	$19.95
2020	Collector's Ency. of Figural & Novelty **Salt & Pepper Shakers**, Vol. II, Davern	$19.95
2018	Collector's Encyclopedia of **Granite Ware**, Greguire	$24.95
3430	Collector's Encyclopedia of **Granite Ware**, Book II, Greguire	$24.95
3879	Collector's Guide to Antique **Radios**, 3rd Ed., Bunis	$18.95
1916	Collector's Guide to **Art Deco**, Gaston	$14.95
3880	Collector's Guide to **Cigarette Lighters**, Flanagan	$17.95
1537	Collector's Guide to **Country Baskets**, Raycraft	$9.95
3966	Collector's Guide to **Inkwells**, Identification & Values, Badders	$18.95
3881	Collector's Guide to **Novelty Radios**, Bunis/Breed	$18.95
3729	Collector's Guide to **Snow Domes**, Guarnaccia	$18.95
3730	Collector's Guide to **Transistor Radios**, Bunis	$15.95
2276	**Decoys**, Kangas	$24.95
1629	**Doorstops**, Identification & Values, Bertoia	$9.95
3968	**Fishing Lure** Collectibles, Murphy/Edmisten	$24.95
3817	**Flea Market Trader**, 9th Ed., Huxford	$12.95
3819	**General Store Collectibles**, Wilson	$24.95
2215	Goldstein's **Coca-Cola** Collectibles	$16.95
3884	Huxford's **Collector's Advertising**, 2nd Ed.	$24.95
2216	**Kitchen Antiques**, 1790–1940, McNerney	$14.95
1782	**1,000 Fruit Jars**, 5th Edition, Schroeder	$5.95
3321	Ornamental & Figural **Nutcrackers**, Rittenhouse	$16.95
2026	**Railroad** Collectibles, 4th Ed., Baker	$14.95
1632	**Salt & Pepper Shakers**, Guarnaccia	$9.95
1888	**Salt & Pepper Shakers** II, Identification & Value Guide, Book II, Guarnaccia	$14.95
2220	**Salt & Pepper Shakers** III, Guarnaccia	$14.95
3443	**Salt & Pepper Shakers** IV, Guarnaccia	$18.95
2096	**Silverplated Flatware**, Revised 4th Edition, Hagan	$14.95
1922	Standard **Old Bottle** Price Guide, Sellari	$14.95
3892	**Toy & Miniature Sewing Machines**, Thomas	$18.95
3828	Value Guide to **Advertising Memorabilia**, Summers	$18.95
3977	Value Guide to **Gas Station** Memorabilia	$24.95
3444	**Wanted to Buy**, 5th Edition	$9.95

Schroeder's
ANTIQUES
Price Guide

. . . is the #1 best-selling antiques & collectibles value guide on the market today, and here's why . . .

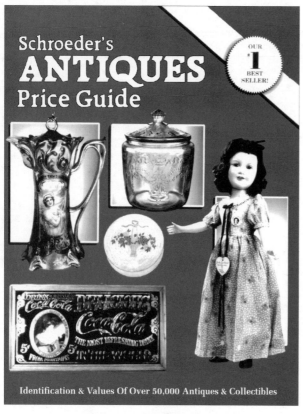

Schroeder's ANTIQUES Price Guide

OUR #1 BEST SELLER!

Identification & Values Of Over 50,000 Antiques & Collectibles

8½ x 11, 608 Pages, $14.95

• *More than 300 advisors, well-known dealers, and top-notch collectors work together with our editors to bring you accurate information regarding pricing and identification.*

• *More than 45,000 items in almost 500 categories are listed along with hundreds of sharp original photos that illustrate not only the rare and unusual, but the common, popular collectibles as well.*

• *Each large close-up shot shows important details clearly. Every subject is represented with histories and background information, a feature not found in any of our competitors' publications.*

• *Our editors keep abreast of newly developing trends, often adding several new categories a year as the need arises.*

If it merits the interest of today's collector, you'll find it in *Schroeder's*. And you can feel confident that the information we publish is up to date and accurate. Our advisors thoroughly check each category to spot inconsistencies, listings that may not be entirely reflective of market dealings, and lines too vague to be of merit. Only the best of the lot remains for publication.

Without doubt, you'll find
SCHROEDER'S ANTIQUES PRICE GUIDE
the only one to buy for
reliable information and values.

COLLECTOR BOOKS
A Division of Schroeder Publishing Co., Inc.